SECOND EDITION

TOP NOTCH

English for Today's World

1B

WITH WORKBOOK

Joan Saslow • Allen Ascher

Top Notch: English for Today's World 1B : عنوان کتاب
with Workbook – 2nd Edition
Joan Saslow, Allen Ascher : مولف
انتشارات جنگل : ناشر
نوبت، سال چاپ : دوم، ۱۳۹۶
قطع، تیراژ : رحلی، ۱۰۰۰
قیمت : ۱۴،۰۰۰ تومان

تهران، میدان انقلاب، خیابان انقلاب، خیابان ۱۲ فروردین، نرسیده به خیابان
منیری جاوید (اردیبهشت)، پلاک ۱۸۵
تلفن : ۶-۰۲۱۶۶۴۹۰۶۴۵ و ۰۲۱۶۶۴۹۰۳۸۲-۴
وب سایت : www.jangal.com
ایمیل : info@junglepub.org

سر شناسه	:	سسلو، جون ام / Saslow, Joan M
عنوان و نام پدید آور	:	Top notch : English for today's world 1B : with workbook Joan Saslow, Allen Ascher With top notch pop songs and karaoke by Rob Morsberger
مشخصات نشر	:	تهران: جنگل، ۱۳۹۳=۲۰۱۴م.
مشخصات ظاهری	:	۱۴۴ص: مصور(بخشی رنگی)، جدول (بخشی رنگی)، عکس؛ ۲۲×۲۹ س م
وضعیت فهرست نویسی	:	فیپا
یادداشت	:	انگلیسی
یادداشت	:	افست از روی ویراست دوم: ۲۰۱۱م.: نیویورک
آوانویسی عنوان	:	تاپ ناچ...
موضوع	:	زبان انگلیسی – کتاب های درسی برای خارجیان
موضوع	:	زبان انگلیسی – آزمون ها و تمرین ها
شناسه افزوده	:	آشر، آلن
شناسه افزوده	:	Ascher, Allen
شناسه افزوده	:	مورسبرگر، رابرت یوستیس، ۱۹۲۹ - م.
شناسه افزوده	:	Morsberger, Robert Eustis
رده بندی کنگره	:	۱۳۹۳ ۲۶۳ت۵س/PE۱۱۲۸ الف
رده بندی دیویی	:	۴۲۸/۲۴
شماره کتابشناسی ملی	:	۳۵۳۷۳۸۵

With *Top Notch Pop Songs and Karaoke*
by Rob Morsberger

PEARSON
Longman

Top Notch: English for Today's World   1B with Workbook, Second Edition

Pearson Education, 10 Bank Street, White Plains, NY 10606

Staff credits: The people who made up the *Top Notch 1* team—representing editorial, design, production, and manufacturing—are Rhea Banker, Elizabeth Carlson, Aerin Csigay, Dave Dickey, Warren Fischbach, Aliza Greenblatt, Ray Keating, Mike Kemper, Barbara Sabella, and Martin Yu.

Cover design: Rhea Banker
Cover photo: Sprint/Corbis
Text design: Elizabeth Carlson and Wendy Wolf
Text composition: Quarasan!
Text font: 9/10 Stone Sans, ITC Stone Sans

Library of Congress Cataloging-in-Publication Data

Saslow, Joan M.
  Top notch : English for today's world / Joan Saslow, Allen Ascher ; with Top Notch pop songs and Karaoke by
  Rob Morsberger. — 2nd ed.
    p. cm.
  ISBN 0-13-246988-X (set) — ISBN 0-13-247038-1 (v. 1) — ISBN 0-13-247048-9 (v. 2) — ISBN 0-13-247027-6
  (v. 3) 1. English language — Textbooks for foreign speakers. 2. English language — Problems, exercises, etc.
  I. Ascher, Allen. II. Title.
PE1128.S2757 2011
428.2'4 — dc22

              2010019162

ISBN 13: 978-0-13-247040-7
ISBN 10: 0-13-247040-3

Photo credits: All original photography by Michal Heron and Sharon Hoogstraten. p. 62 (top) PhotoDisc/Getty Images, (bottom) Shutterstock.com; p. 63 (background) iStockphoto.com, (top right) Radius Images/Alamy; p. 65 (bottom) Shutterstock.com; p. 66 (park) Rudi Von Briel/PhotoEdit, Inc., (gym) David Sacks/Getty Images, (track) Tom Carter/PhotoEdit, Inc., (pool) Pat Lanza/Bruce Coleman Inc., (field) Sergio Piumatti, (course) Dorling Kindersley, (court) R.W. Jones/Corbis; p. 70 (top right) Handout/Getty Images, (left) Bob Daemmrich/Corbis (bottom right) Noah Hamilton; p. 74 (London) Shutterstock.com, (Paris) Shutterstock.com, (Rome) Louis A. Goldman/Photo Researchers, Inc., (Vienna) Javier Larrea/Photolibrary, (Copenhagen) Dreamstime.com, (boat) Shutterstock.com, (windsurf) Shutterstock.com, (snorkel) Bill Varie/Corbis; p. 75 (bottom) Shutterstock.com; p. 76 (background) iStockphoto.com; p. 77 iStockphoto.com; p. 78 Shutterstock.com; p. 79 (Perth) Dorling Kindersley, (Egypt) Shutterstock.com, (New York) Shutterstock.com, (Buenos) Imagebroker/Alamy; p. 80 (left) Gabe Rogel/Getty Images, (middle) Luca Tettoni/Corbis, (right) HFHI/David Snyder; p. 81 (left) Shutterstock.com, (middle right) Shutterstock.com, (right) Shutterstock.com; p. 85 (background) Shutterstock.com; p. 86 (jackets) Dorling Kindersley, (sweaters) Shutterstock.com (boxers) Comstock Royalty Free Division, (bras) Shutterstock.com, (purses) Dorling Kindersley, (belts) Richard Megna/Fundamental Photographs, (bathrobes) Comstock Royalty Free Division, (shoes) Siede Preis/Getty Images; p. 89 (top left) Shutterstock.com, (top right) Shutterstock.com; p. 94 (travelin) Shutterstock.com, (jillian) Shutterstock.com, (tall) Shutterstock.com, (middle right) LOOK Die Bildagentur der Fotografen GmbH/Alamy; p. 95 Shutterstock.com; p. 98 Shutterstock.com; p. 99 (background left) iStockphoto.com, (background middle) Shutterstock.com, (background right) iStockphoto.com; p. 104 Shutterstock.com; p. 105 (top) Mike Powell/Getty Images, (bottom) Gogo Images/Photolibrary; p. 106 Shutterstock.com; p. 110 (left) iStockphoto.com, (middle) Shutterstock.com, (right) Shutterstock.com; p. 115 (bowls) Shutterstock.com, (vase) Photos.com, (sunglasses) Shutterstock.com, (hat) Dorling Kindersley/Getty Images, (sweater) iStockphoto.com; p. 116 (left) Jamie Grill/Photolibrary, (right) Joshua Ets-Hokin/Photolibrary; p. 117 (left) Shutterstock.com, (middle right) Shutterstock.com, (right) Shutterstock.com; p. 118 (middle) Shutterstock.com, (bottom) Shutterstock.com; p. 119 Shutterstock.com; p. W50 Richard T. Nowitz/Corbis; p. W60 Shutterstock.com; p. W62 Phil Cantor/Index Stock Imagery; p. W63 Bill Bachmann/Index Stock Imagery; p. W68 Shutterstock.com; p. W69 (1) Shutterstock.com, (2) Shutterstock.com, (3) Shutterstock.com, (4) Photos.com, (5) iStockphoto.com, (6) Shutterstock.com; p. W72 (3 left) Silver Burdett Ginn/Pearson, (3 right) Getty Images; p. W75 (left) Jess Stock/Getty Images, (middle left) Dorling Kindersley, (middle right) Thomas Craig/Index Stock Imagery, (right) Shutterstock.com; p. W81 Shutterstock.com; p. W92 Bloomberg/Getty Images.

Illustration credits: Kenneth Batelman, pp. 88, 92, 93, 100, 107; Pierre Berthiaume, p. W82; Rich Burlew, pp. 62, W50; John Ceballos, pp. 85, 109; Bob Doucet, p. 97; Leanne Franson, pp. W61, W71; Scott Fray, p. W72; Steve Gardner, p. W89; Marty Harris, p. 77; Brian Hughes, pp. 106 (center), 113, W87; Jim Kopp, p. 104; André Labrie, p. W72; Adam Larkum, p. 73; Andy Meyer, pp. 106 (top), W81, W82; Suzanne Morgensen, p. W79; Sandy Nichols, pp. 80, 102; NSV Productions, pp. W85, W86; Dusan Petricic, pp. 82, 83, 118, W65, W82; Michel Rabagliati, p. 70; Robert Schoolcraft, p. 121; XNR Productions, 74, 75, 106 (bottom).

Printed in the United States of America
1 2 3 4 5 6 7 8 9 10 – V042 – 15 14 13 12 11 10

CONTENTS

Learning Objectives

Top Notch 1 learning objectives are designed for false beginners. They offer a rigorous review and an expansion of key beginning concepts as well as a wealth of new and challenging material.

Unit	Communication Goals	Vocabulary	Grammar
1 **Getting Acquainted** page 2	• Meet someone new • Identify and describe people • Provide personal information • Introduce someone to a group	• Usage of formal titles • Positive adjectives to describe people • Personal information • Countries and nationalities	• Information questions with <u>be</u> (review and common errors) • Modification with adjectives (review) • <u>Yes</u> / <u>no</u> questions and short answers with <u>be</u> (review) **GRAMMAR BOOSTER** • <u>Be</u>: usage and form (review) • <u>Be</u>: common errors • Possessive nouns and adjectives (review)
2 **Going Out** page 14	• Accept or decline an invitation • Express locations and give directions • Make plans to see an event • Talk about musical tastes	• Music genres • Entertainment and cultural events • Locations and directions	• Prepositions of time and place • Questions with <u>When</u>, <u>What time</u>, and <u>Where</u> (review) **GRAMMAR BOOSTER** • Prepositions of time and place: usage

3
The Extended Family
page 26
	• Report news about relationships
	• Describe extended families
	• Compare people
	• Discuss family cultural traditions
		• Extended family relationships
		• Marital status
		• Relatives by marriage
		• Describing similarities and differences
			• The simple present tense (review):
			  ○ Affirmative and negative statements
			  ○ <u>Yes</u> / <u>no</u> questions
			  ○ Information questions
			  ○ Common errors
			GRAMMAR BOOSTER
			• The simple present tense:
			  ○ Usage, form, common errors
			  ○ Questions with <u>Who</u>

4 **Food and Restaurants** page 38	• Ask for a restaurant recommendation • Order from a menu • Speak to a server and pay for a meal • Discuss food and health	• Parts of a meal • Categories of food and drink • Communicating with a waiter or waitress • Adjectives to describe the healthfulness of food	• <u>There is</u> and <u>there are</u> with count and non-count nouns • <u>Anything</u> and <u>nothing</u>: common errors • Definite article <u>the</u>: usage **GRAMMAR BOOSTER** • Non-count nouns: usage, expressing quantities • <u>How much</u> / <u>How many</u> • Count nouns: Spelling rules • <u>Some</u> and <u>any</u>

5
Technology and You
page 50
	• Suggest a brand or model
	• Express frustration and sympathy
	• Describe features of products
	• Complain when things don't work
		• Electronic products
		• Household appliances and machines
		• Features of manufactured products
		• Ways to state a problem
		• Ways to sympathize
		• Positive and negative adjectives
			• The present continuous (review):
			  ○ Actions in progress and future plans
			  ○ Statements and questions
			GRAMMAR BOOSTER
			• The present continuous: form and spelling rules

Conversation Strategies	Listening/Pronunciation	Reading	Writing
• Begin responses with a question to confirm • Use <u>Let's</u> to suggest a course of action • Ask personal questions to indicate friendliness • Intensify an informal answer with <u>sure</u>	**Listening Skills:** • Listen for details • Infer information **Pronunciation:** • Intonation of questions	**Texts:** • An enrollment form • Personal profiles • A photo story **Skills/strategies:** • Infer information • Scan for facts	**Task:** • Write a description of a classmate **WRITING BOOSTER** • Capitalization
• Use <u>Really?</u> to express enthusiasm • Provide reasons to decline an invitation • Use <u>Too bad</u> to express disappointment • Repeat with rising intonation to confirm information • Use <u>Thanks, anyway</u> to acknowledge an unsuccessful attempt to help	**Listening Skills:** • Infer a speaker's intention • Listen for main ideas • Listen for details • Listen for locations **Pronunciation:** • Rising intonation to confirm information	**Texts:** • A music website • An entertainment events page • Authentic interviews • A survey of musical tastes • A photo story **Skills/strategies:** • Interpret maps and diagrams • Identify supporting details • Make personal comparisons	**Task:** • Write a short personal essay about one's musical tastes **WRITING BOOSTER** • The sentence
• Use <u>Actually</u> to introduce a topic • Respond to good news with <u>Congratulations!</u> • Respond to bad news with <u>I'm sorry to hear that</u> • Use <u>Thanks for asking</u> to acknowledge an inquiry of concern • Use <u>Well</u> to introduce a lengthy reply • Ask follow-up questions to keep a conversation going	**Listening Skills:** • Infer information • Understand key details • Identify similarities and differences • Listen to take notes • Listen for main ideas • Listen for details **Pronunciation:** • Blending sounds	**Texts:** • Family tree diagrams • A self-help website • A cultural-information survey • A photo story **Skills/strategies:** • Interpret a diagram • Confirm facts • Infer information	**Task:** • Make a Venn diagram • Compare two people in a family **WRITING BOOSTER** • Combining sentences with <u>and</u> or <u>but</u>
• Use <u>Could you ...?</u> to make a polite request • Use <u>Sure</u> to agree to a request • Clarify a request by asking for more specific information • Indicate a sudden thought with <u>Actually</u> • Use <u>I'll have</u> to order from a server • Increase politeness with <u>please</u>	**Listening Skills:** • Listen to take notes • Infer the location of a conversation • Listen to predict **Pronunciation:** • <u>The</u> before consonant and vowel sounds	**Texts:** • Menus • A nutrition website • A photo story **Skills/strategies:** • Interpret a map • Understand from context • Infer information	**Task:** • Write a short article about food for a travel newsletter **WRITING BOOSTER** • Connecting words and ideas: <u>and, in addition</u>
• Use <u>Hey</u> or <u>How's it going</u> for an informal greeting • Use <u>What about...?</u> to offer a suggestion • Use <u>Really?</u> to indicate surprise • Use <u>You know</u> to introduce a topic • Express sympathy when someone is frustrated	**Listening Skills:** • Listen to predict • Infer meaning • Listen for details **Pronunciation:** • Intonation of questions	**Texts:** • Newspaper advertisements • A magazine ad for a new product • A photo story **Skills/strategies:** • Understand from context • Activate language from a text	**Task:** • Write a paragraph describing a product **WRITING BOOSTER** • Placement of adjectives

Unit	Communication Goals	Vocabulary	Grammar
6 **Staying in Shape** page 62	• Plan an activity with someone • Talk about habitual activities • Discuss fitness and eating habits • Describe someone's routines	• Physical activities • Places for physical activities • Frequency adverbs: expansion	• <u>Can</u> and <u>have to</u>: meaning, form, and usage • The present continuous and the simple present tense (review) • The present continuous: common errors **GRAMMAR BOOSTER** • Non-action verbs • Frequency adverbs: common errors • Time expressions • More on <u>can</u> and <u>have to</u>
7 **On Vacation** page 74	• Greet someone arriving from a trip • Ask about someone's vacation • Discuss vacation preferences • Describe good and bad travel experiences	• Adjectives to describe trips and vacations • Intensifiers • Ways to describe good and bad travel experiences	• The past tense of <u>be</u> (review): statements and questions • The simple past tense (review): statements and questions • Regular and irregular verb forms **GRAMMAR BOOSTER** • The past tense of <u>be</u>: explanation of form • The simple past tense: more on spelling, usage, and form
8 **Shopping for Clothes** page 86	• Shop and pay for clothes • Ask for a different size or color • Navigate a mall or department store • Discuss clothing do's and don'ts	• Clothing departments • Types of clothing and shoes • Clothing that comes in "pairs" • Interior store locations and directions • Formality and appropriateness in clothing	• Uses of object pronouns • Object pronouns: common errors • Comparative adjectives **GRAMMAR BOOSTER** • Direct and indirect objects: usage rules • Spelling rules for comparative adjectives
9 **Taking Transportation** page 98	• Discuss schedules and buy tickets • Book travel services • Understand airport announcements • Describe transportation problems	• Kinds of tickets and trips • Travel services • Airline passenger information • Flight problems • Transportation problems • Means of public transportation	• Modals <u>should</u> and <u>could</u>: statements and questions • <u>Be going to</u> to express the future: review and expansion **GRAMMAR BOOSTER** • Modals: form, meaning, common errors • Expansion: future actions
10 **Shopping Smart** page 110	• Ask for a recommendation • Bargain for a lower price • Discuss showing appreciation for service • Describe where to get the best deals	• Financial terms • How to bargain • How to describe good and bad deals	• Superlative adjectives • <u>Too</u> and <u>enough</u>: usage and common errors **GRAMMAR BOOSTER** • Superlative adjectives: usage and form • Comparatives (review) • Usage: <u>very</u>, <u>really</u>, and <u>too</u>

Conversation Strategies	Listening/ Pronunciation	Reading	Writing
• Use <u>Why don't we . . . ?</u> to suggest an activity • Say <u>Sorry, I can't</u> to apologize for turning down an invitation • Provide a reason with <u>have to</u> to decline an invitation • Use <u>Well, how about . . . ?</u> to suggest an alternative • Use <u>How come?</u> to ask for a reason • Use a negative question to confirm information	**Listening Skills:** • Infer meaning • Infer information • Listen for main ideas • Listen for details • Apply and personalize information **Pronunciation:** • <u>Can</u> / <u>can't</u> • The third-person singular <u>-s</u>	**Texts:** • A bar graph • A fitness survey • A magazine article • A photo story **Skills/strategies:** • Interpret a bar graph • Infer information • Summarize	**Task:** • Write an interview about health and exercise habits **WRITING BOOSTER** • Punctuation of statements and questions
• Say <u>Welcome back!</u> to indicate enthusiasm about someone's return from a trip • Acknowledge someone's interest with <u>Actually</u> • Decline an offer of assistance with <u>That's OK. I'm fine.</u> • Confirm that an offer is declined with <u>Are you sure?</u> • Use <u>Absolutely</u> to confirm a response • Show enthusiasm with <u>No kidding!</u> and <u>Tell me more</u>	**Listening Skills:** • Listen for main ideas • Listen for details • Infer meaning **Pronunciation:** • The simple past tense ending: regular verbs	**Texts:** • Travel brochures • Personal travel stories • A vacation survey • A photo story **Skills/strategies:** • Activate language from a text • Draw conclusions • Identify supporting details	**Task:** • Write a guided essay about a vacation **WRITING BOOSTER** • Time order
• Use <u>Excuse me</u> to indicate you didn't understand or couldn't hear • Use <u>Excuse me</u> to begin a conversation with a clerk • Follow a question with more information for clarification • Acknowledge someone's assistance with <u>Thanks for your help</u> • Respond to gratitude with <u>My pleasure</u>	**Listening Skills:** • Infer the appropriate location • Infer the locations of conversations • Understand locations and directions **Pronunciation:** • Contrastive stress for clarification	**Texts:** • A clothing catalogue • Simple and complex diagrams and plans • A travel blog • A personal opinion survey • A photo story **Skills/strategies:** • Paraphrase • Identify supporting details • Apply information	**Task:** • Write an e-mail or letter explaining what clothes to pack **WRITING BOOSTER** • Connecting ideas with <u>because</u> and <u>since</u>
• Use <u>I'm sorry</u> to respond with disappointing information • Use <u>Well</u> to introduce an alternative. • Use <u>I hope so</u> to politely respond to an offer of help • Use <u>Let me check</u> to buy time to get information	**Listening Skills:** • Infer the type of travel service • Understand public announcements • Listen for details • Use reasoning to evaluate statements of fact **Pronunciation:** • Intonation for stating alternatives	**Texts:** • Transportation schedules • Public transportation tickets • Arrival and departure boards • Newspaper articles • A photo story **Skills/strategies:** • Make decisions based on schedules and needs • Critical thinking	**Task:** • Write two paragraphs about trips **WRITING BOOSTER** • The paragraph
• Use <u>Well</u> to connect an answer to an earlier question • Use <u>How about . . . ?</u> to make a financial offer • Use <u>OK</u> to indicate that an agreement has been reached	**Listening Skills:** • Listen for details • Listen for main ideas **Pronunciation:** • Rising intonation for clarification	**Texts:** • A travel guide • A magazine article • Personal travel stories • A photo story **Skills/strategies:** • Draw conclusions • Apply information	**Task:** • Write a guide to your city, including information on where to stay, visit, and shop **WRITING BOOSTER** • Connecting contradictory ideas: <u>even though</u>, <u>however</u>, <u>on the other hand</u>

What is *Top Notch*?

Top Notch is a six-level* communicative course that prepares adults and young adults to interact successfully and confidently with both native and non-native speakers of English.

The goal of the *Top Notch* course is to make English unforgettable through:

► Multiple exposures to new language
► Numerous opportunities to practice it
► Deliberate and intensive recycling

The *Top Notch* course has two beginning levels: *Top Notch* Fundamentals for true beginners and *Top Notch* 1 for false beginners.

Each full level of *Top Notch* contains enough material for 60 to 90 hours of classroom instruction. A wide choice of supplementary components makes it easy to tailor *Top Notch* to the needs of your classes.

Summit 1 and *Summit* 2 are the titles of the fifth and sixth levels of the *Top Notch* course. All Student's Books are available in split editions with bound-in workbooks.

The *Top Notch* instructional design

Daily confirmation of progress

Each easy-to-follow two-page lesson begins with a clearly stated communication goal. All lesson activities are integrated with the goal and systematically build toward a final speaking activity in which students demonstrate achievement of the goal. "Can-do" statements in each unit ensure students' awareness of the continuum of their progress.

A purposeful conversation syllabus

Memorable conversation models provide essential and practical social language that students can carry "in their pockets" for use in real life. Guided conversation pair work enables students to modify, personalize, and extend each model so they can use it to communicate their own thoughts and needs. Free discussion activities are carefully crafted so students can continually retrieve and use the language from the models. All conversation models are informed by the Longman Corpus of Spoken American English.

An emphasis on cultural fluency

Recognizing that English is a global language, *Top Notch* actively equips students to interact socially with people from a variety of cultures and deliberately prepares them to understand accented speakers from diverse language backgrounds.

Intensive vocabulary development

Students actively work with a rich vocabulary of high-frequency words, collocations, and expressions in all units of the Student's Book. Clear illustrations and definitions clarify meaning and provide support for independent study, review, and test preparation. Systematic recycling promotes smooth and continued acquisition of vocabulary from the beginning to the advanced levels of the course.

A dynamic approach to grammar

An explicit grammar syllabus is supported by charts containing clear grammar rules, relevant examples, and explanations of meaning and use. Numerous grammar exercises provide focused practice, and grammar usage is continually activated in communication exercises that illustrate the grammar being learned.

A dedicated pronunciation syllabus

Focused pronunciation, rhythm, and intonation practice is included in each unit, providing application of each pronunciation point to the target language of the unit and facilitating comprehensible pronunciation.

ActiveBook

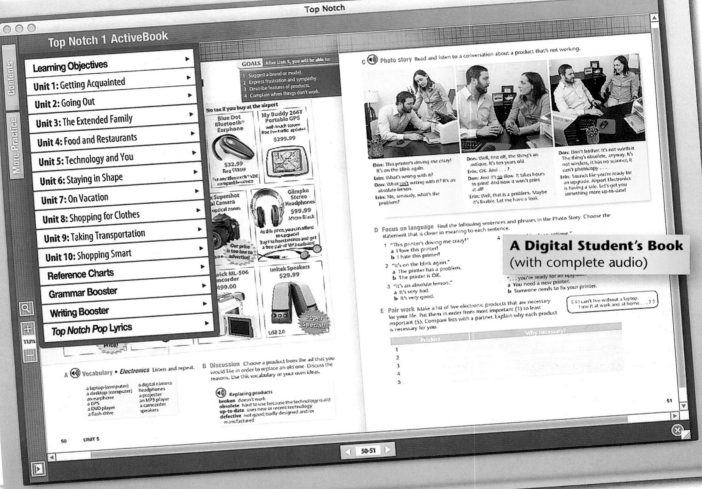

Top Notch 1 ActiveBook

Contents

- Learning Objectives
- Unit 1: Getting Acquainted
- Unit 2: Going Out
- Unit 3: The Extended Family
- Unit 4: Food and Restaurants
- Unit 5: Technology and You
- Unit 6: Staying in Shape
- Unit 7: On Vacation
- Unit 8: Shopping for Clothes
- Unit 9: Taking Transportation
- Unit 10: Shopping Smart
- Reference Charts
- Grammar Booster
- Writing Booster
- Top Notch Pop Lyrics

A Digital Student's Book
(with complete audio)

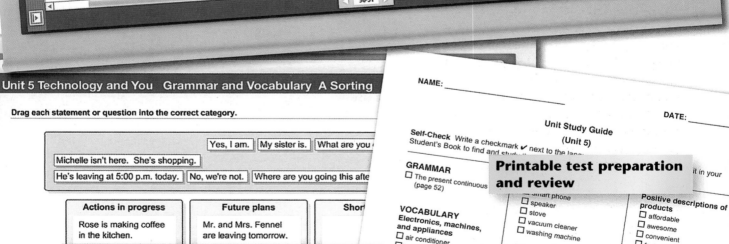

Interactive practice (with daily activity records)
- ▶ Extra listening and reading comprehension
- ▶ Record-yourself speaking
- ▶ Grammar and vocabulary practice
- ▶ Games and puzzles
- ▶ *Top Notch Pop* and karaoke

Printable test preparation and review

ix

The Teacher's Edition and Lesson Planner

Includes:

- ► A bound-in Methods Handbook for professional development
- ► Detailed lesson plans with suggested teaching times
- ► Language, culture, and corpus notes
- ► Student's Book and Workbook answer keys
- ► Audioscripts
- ► *Top Notch TV* teaching notes

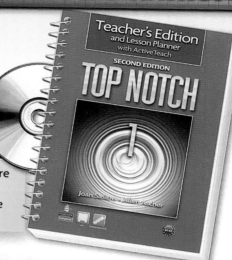

► ActiveTeach

- ► A Digital Student's Book with interactive whiteboard (IWB) software
- ► Instantly accessible audio and *Top Notch TV* video
- ► Interactive exercises from the Student's *ActiveBook* for in-class use
- ► A complete menu of printable extension activities

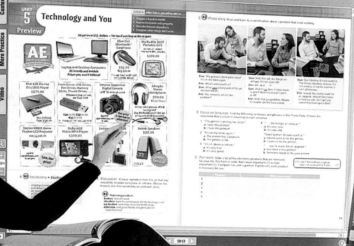

Top Notch TV

A hilarious situation comedy, authentic unrehearsed on-the-street interviews, and *Top Notch Pop* karaoke.

The Digital Student's Book
With zoom, write, highlight, save and other IWB tools.

Printable Extension Activities
Including:
- Writing process worksheets
- Vocabulary flashcards
- Learning strategies
- Graphic organizers
- Pronunciation activities
- Video activity worksheets and more . . .

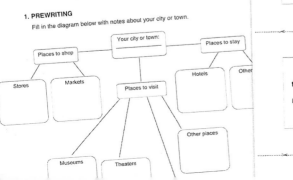

Page 1 of 2

NAME: _____ DATE: _____

Writing Process Worksheet
(Accompanies Unit 10, page 120)

ASSIGNMENT: Write a guide about the places for a visitor to your city or town to stay in, visit, and shop.

1. PREWRITING
Fill in the diagram below with notes about your city or town.

Electronics

Electronics

NAME: _____

Learning Strategy
(Unit 6, page 70, Reading)

READING STRATEGY: skimming

When you read an article, skim for the main ideas first before you read for details.

In the article below, the unimportant parts have been deleted. Notice how much you can understand with fewer words in the article.

When You Think You Can't . . .
Mark Zupan

▧ — — accident in 1993 — Mark Zupan - quadriplegic — changed his life — — cannot move — arms or legs —

— — — plays quad rugby— — — — — — winning a gold medal in — 2008 — — —, — — —,

—, — gives talks — raises money for his sport. — — — —, — —
lifts weights — — — — —, drives a car, goes to rock concerts. — — — —

— careful about — diet — — —
—,— —,

Bethany Hamilton
▧ — Bethany Hamilton — — — —, — — in 2003, she lost her — arm — — attacked by - shark — Three weeks later

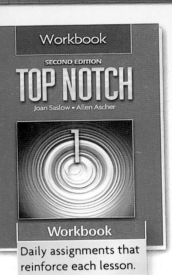

Workbook

Daily assignments that reinforce each lesson.

Classroom Audio Program

Includes a variety of authentic regional and non-native accents.

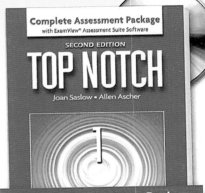

Complete Assessment Package

Ready-made achievement tests. Software provides option to edit, delete, or add items.

Full-Course Placement Tests

Choose printable or online version.

Copy & Go

Board games, role plays, information gaps, and "find someone who. . ." for every lesson.

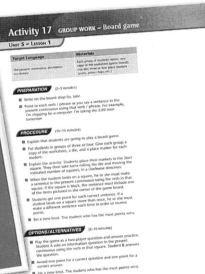

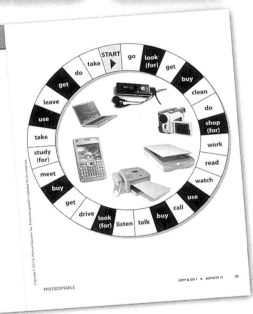

MyTopNotchLab

An optional online learning tool with:

► An interactive *Top Notch* Workbook
► Speaking and writing activities
► Pop-up grammar help
► Student's Book *Grammar Booster* exercises
► *Top Notch TV* with extensive viewing activities
► Automatically-graded achievement tests
► Easy course management and record-keeping

Staying in Shape

GOALS After Unit 6, you will be abl

1 Plan an activity with someone.
2 Talk about habitual activities.
3 Discuss fitness and eating habits.
4 Describe someone's routines.

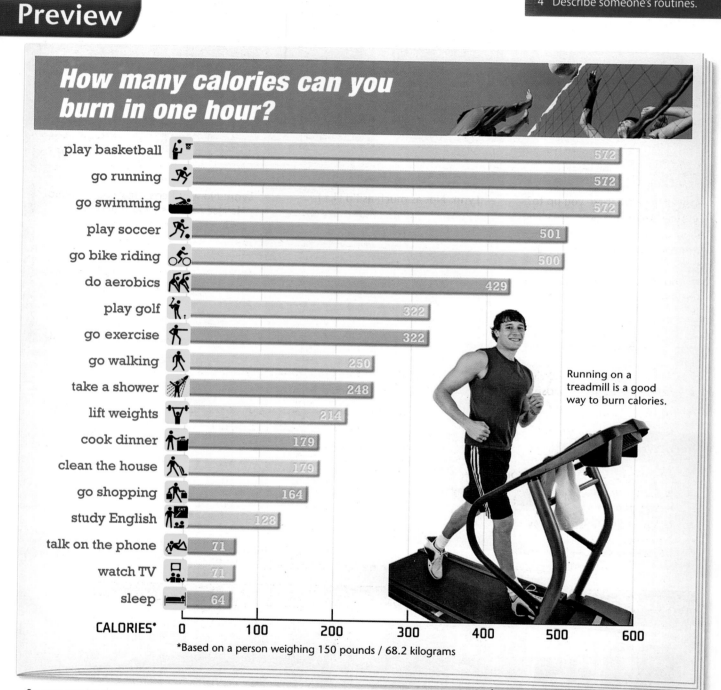

How many calories can you burn in one hour?

Activity	Calories
play basketball	572
go running	572
go swimming	572
play soccer	501
go bike riding	500
do aerobics	429
play golf	322
go exercise	322
go walking	250
take a shower	248
lift weights	214
cook dinner	179
clean the house	179
go shopping	164
study English	128
talk on the phone	71
watch TV	71
sleep	64

CALORIES* 0 100 200 300 400 500 600

*Based on a person weighing 150 pounds / 68.2 kilograms

Running on a treadmill is a good way to burn calories.

Source: msnbc.com

A 3:24 ◀)) **Vocabulary • *Activities*** Listen and repeat.

B **Class survey** According to the graph, approximately how many calories do <u>you</u> burn every day? Find out who in your class burns more than 1500 calories a day.

C 🔊 **3:25 Photo story** Read and listen to people talking about playing tennis.

Lynn: Hi, Joy! What are you up to?

Joy: Lynn! How are you? I'm playing tennis, actually. In the park.

Lynn: You play tennis? I didn't know that.

Joy: I do. About three times a week. Do you play?

Lynn: Not as much as I'd like to.

Joy: Well, why don't we make a date to play sometime?

Lynn: That would be great.

Joy: Hey, how about your husband? Would he like to come, too?

Lynn: No way. Ken's a real couch potato. He just watches TV and eats junk food. He's so out of shape.

Joy: Too bad. My husband's crazy about tennis.

Lynn: Listen. I'm on my way home right now. Let's talk next week. OK?

Joy: Terrific.

D Focus on language Look at the underlined expressions in the Photo Story. Use the context to help you choose the correct meaning of the following sentences.

1 What are you up to?
   a What are you doing?
   b Where are you going?

2 Why don't we play tennis sometime?
   a Can you explain why we don't play tennis?
   b Would you like to play tennis sometime?

3 My husband is really out of shape.
   a My husband doesn't exercise.
   b My husband exercises a lot.

4 I'm crazy about tennis.
   a I hate tennis.
   b I love tennis.

E Personalize Review time expressions. Look at page 62. List the activities you do . . .

every day	every weekend	once a week	once in a while	never

F Pair work Compare activities with a partner.

❝ What do you do every weekend? ❞

❝ Me? I go shopping. ❞

GOAL   Plan an activity with someone

GRAMMAR   Can and have to

can
Use can + the base form of a verb for possibility.

I can go out for dinner tonight. I don't have class in the morning.
I can't play golf today. I'm too busy.
She can meet us at the park, but her husband can't.
Can you go running tomorrow at three? (Yes, I can. / No, I can't.)

Remember: can + base form also expresses ability.
We **can speak** English.
They **can't play** piano.

have to
Use have to or has to + the base form of a verb for obligation.

She $\left\{\begin{array}{l}\text{has to} \\ \text{doesn't have to}\end{array}\right\}$ meet her cousin at the airport.

They $\left\{\begin{array}{l}\text{have to} \\ \text{don't have to}\end{array}\right\}$ work late tonight.

Do you have to work tomorrow? (Yes, I do. / No, I don't.)
Does he have to go to class? (Yes, he does. / No, he doesn't.)

Usage: When declining an invitation, use have to to provide a reason.
Sorry, I **can't. I have to work** late.

GRAMMAR BOOSTER ▸ p. 131

Can and _have to_:
• Form and common errors
• Information questions
Can and _be able to_:
• Present and past forms

A Grammar practice Read the sentences carefully. Then complete each sentence with can or have to.

1 I'd like to go out tonight, but we have a test tomorrow. I ....
                                                                        study

2 Audrey .... us for lunch today. She .... her boss write a report.
               not / meet   help

3 Good news! I .... late tonight. We .... together at 6:00.
                    not / work   go running

4 My sister .... at the mall today. She .... to the doctor.
               not / go shopping   go

5 Henry .... to Toronto next week, so he .... golf with us.
           go   not / play

B Pair work On a separate sheet of paper, write three questions using can and three questions using have to. Then practice asking and answering the questions with a partner.

PRONUNCIATION   Can / can't

A 🔊 **3:26** Listen to the pronunciation and stress of can and can't in sentences. Then listen again and repeat.

I **can call** you today.   I **can't call** you tomorrow.

/kən/   /kænt/

B 🔊 **3:27** Listen to the statements and check can or can't. Then listen again and repeat each statement.

1 ☐ can   ☐ can't   3 ☐ can   ☐ can't   5 ☐ can   ☐ can't
2 ☐ can   ☐ can't   4 ☐ can   ☐ can't   6 ☐ can   ☐ can't

A 🔊 3:28 Read and listen to two people planning an activity together.

A: Hey, Phil. Why don't we go bike riding sometime?

B: Great idea. When's good for you?

A: Tomorrow at 3:00?

B: Sorry, I can't. I have to meet my sister at the airport.

A: Well, how about Sunday afternoon at 2:00?

B: That sounds fine. See you then.

B 🔊 3:29 **Rhythm and intonation** Listen again and repeat. Then practice the Conversation Model with a partner.

NOW YOU CAN   Plan an activity with someone

A Write your schedule for this weekend in the daily planner.

	Friday	Saturday	Sunday
9:00	go running	visit Mom	

Daily Planner

	Friday	Saturday	Sunday
9:00			
11:00			
1:00			
3:00			
5:00			
7:00			

B Pair work Now change the Conversation Model, using your daily planner. Then change roles.

A: Hey, ... Why don't we .... sometime?

B: .... When's good for you?

A: ....?

B: Sorry, I can't. I have to ....

A: Well, how about ....?

B: ....

Don't stop!
- Make more excuses using can't and have to.
- Suggest other activities you can do together. (Use page 62 for ideas.)
- Discuss where to meet.

C Change partners Plan other activities. Use your daily planner to respond.

GOAL **Talk about habitual activities**

Places for physical activities

A 🔊 3:30 Read and listen. Then listen again and repeat.

a park

a gym

a track

a pool

an athletic field

a golf course

a tennis court

B **Pair work** Tell your partner what you do at these places.

> ❝I play soccer at the athletic field next to the school.❞

GRAMMAR *The present continuous and the simple present tense: Review*

The present continuous
(for actions in progress and future plans)

I'm making dinner right now.
They're swimming at the pool in the park.
He's meeting his friends for lunch tomorrow.

The simple present tense
(for frequency, habits, and routines)

I make dinner at least twice a week.
They usually swim at the pool on Tuesdays.
He hardly ever meets his friends for dinner.

Be careful!
Don't use the present continuous with frequency adverbs.
Don't say: ~~She's never playing tennis.~~
Don't use the present continuous with have, want, need, or like.
Don't say: ~~She's liking the gym.~~

GRAMMAR BOOSTER ▸ p. 133
• *Non-action verbs*
• *Placement of frequency adverbs*
• *Time expressions*

🔊 3:31 **Frequency adverbs**
100%   always
↑   almost always
        usually / often / generally
        sometimes / occasionally
        hardly ever
0%   never

A Grammar practice Complete the sentences. Use the simple present tense or the present continuous.

1 Brian can't answer the phone right now.
....
      He / study

2 How often .... walking?
            she / go

3 .... tennis this weekend.
    We / play

4 .... weights three times a week.
    He / lift

5 .... lunch. Can they call you back?
    They / make

6 How often .... the house?
           you / clean

7 .... aerobics every day.
      I / do

8 .... shopping tonight.
    She / go

B 🔊 3:32 **Listening comprehension** Listen to the conversations. Circle the frequency adverb that best completes each statement.

1 She (often / hardly ever / never) plays golf.

2 He (often / sometimes / always) goes to the gym four times a week.

3 She (often / sometimes / never) plays tennis in the park.

4 He (always / often / never) goes swimming.

5 She (always / sometimes / never) rides her bike on weekends.

CONVERSATION MODEL

A 🔊 3:33 Read and listen to two people talking about habitual activities.

A: Hey, Nancy. Where are you off to?

B: Hi, Trish. I'm going to the gym.

A: Really? Don't you usually go there on weekends?

B: Yes. But not <u>this</u> weekend.

A: How come?

B: Because this weekend I'm going to the beach.

B 🔊 3:34 **Rhythm and intonation** Listen again and repeat. Then practice the Conversation Model with a partner.

C Find the grammar Look at the Conversation Model again. Underline one example of the simple present tense and two examples of the present continuous. Which one has future meaning?

NOW YOU CAN | Talk about habitual activities

A Pair work Now change the Conversation Model, using places from the Vocabulary or other places. Then change roles.

A: Hey, ... Where are you off to?

B: Hi, ... I'm going to the ....

A: Really? Don't you usually go there on ....?

B: Yes. But not this ....

A: How come?

B: Because .... I'm ....

> **Don't stop!**
> • Ask about the activities your partner does. What do you do at the ___?
> • Invite your partner to do something. Why don't we ___ sometime?

B Change partners Practice the conversation again. Use a different place and activity.

GOAL   **Discuss fitness and eating habits**

Warm-up In your opinion, is it important for people to stay in shape? Why? What do people have to do to stay in shape?

A ◀)) **Listen for main ideas** Listen to people talking about their fitness and eating habits. Check the box if the person exercises regularly.

☐ **Jessica Miller**

☐ **Juan Reyneri**

☐ **Naomi Sato**

B ◀)) **Listen for details** Now listen again and circle the words that complete the statements.

Jessica Miller (walks / runs / swims) to stay in shape. She tries to avoid (fatty / salty / spicy) foods. She likes desserts, but she avoids (candy / chocolate / cookies). She always drinks a lot of (soda / juice / water).

To stay in shape, Juan Reyneri goes running and (does aerobics / lifts weights / goes swimming). He eats five or six (small / medium / large) meals each day. He usually avoids sodas and (chips / sweets / fries). He (often / occasionally / never) eats junk food.

Naomi Sato sometimes goes (walking / running / swimming). She doesn't have much time to (cook / exercise / eat). She eats (fish / meat / vegetables) once a week and lots of (soup / candy / salads).

C Discussion

  1 Which of the people above do you think are in shape or out of shape? Explain.

  2 Whose fitness and eating habits are like your own? Explain.

  Third-person singular –s: Review

A ◀)) Read and listen to the three third-person singular endings. Then listen again and repeat.

/s/	/z/	/ɪz/
sleeps	goes	watches
eats	plays	exercises
works	avoids	munches

B Pair work Take turns reading the statements in Exercise B. Listen for details, practicing third-person singular endings.

A **Frame your ideas** Take the health survey.

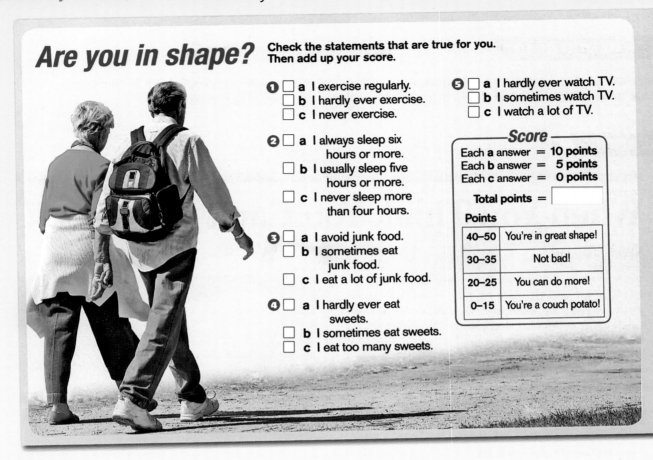

Are you in shape?

Check the statements that are true for you.
Then add up your score.

1
- [ ] **a** I exercise regularly.
- [ ] **b** I hardly ever exercise.
- [ ] **c** I never exercise.

2
- [ ] **a** I always sleep six hours or more.
- [ ] **b** I usually sleep five hours or more.
- [ ] **c** I never sleep more than four hours.

3
- [ ] **a** I avoid junk food.
- [ ] **b** I sometimes eat junk food.
- [ ] **c** I eat a lot of junk food.

4
- [ ] **a** I hardly ever eat sweets.
- [ ] **b** I sometimes eat sweets.
- [ ] **c** I eat too many sweets.

5
- [ ] **a** I hardly ever watch TV.
- [ ] **b** I sometimes watch TV.
- [ ] **c** I watch a lot of TV.

Score

Each **a** answer = **10 points**
Each **b** answer = **5 points**
Each **c** answer = **0 points**

Total points = _____

Points

40–50	You're in great shape!
30–35	Not bad!
20–25	You can do more!
0–15	You're a couch potato!

B **Pair work** Compare your answers and scores on the survey.

C **Group work** Walk around the classroom and ask questions. Write names and take notes on the chart.

Don't stop!
Ask for more information.

Why are you out of shape?
What junk foods do you eat?
Where do you exercise?

Find someone who . . .	Name	Other information
is in great shape.	Dan	goes running every day

Find someone who . . .	Name	Other information
is in great shape.		
is out of shape.		
eats a lot of junk food.		
avoids sweets.		
avoids fatty foods.		
never sleeps more than four hours.		

D **Discussion** Now discuss fitness and eating habits. Tell your classmates about the people on your chart.

" Dan is in great shape. He goes running every day. "

GOAL   **Describe someone's routines**

Preview Look only at the titles, photos, and captions. What do these two people have in common? What do you think they have to do in order to participate successfully in their sports?

When You Think You Can't . . .

Mark Zupan

A terrible accident in 1993 made Mark Zupan a quadriplegic and changed his life forever. He cannot move his arms or legs normally, and he has to take medication so his legs don't shake. However, after a lot of hard work, he can now use his arms to move his wheelchair, and he can even stand for a short time and take a few slow steps. Zupan—or Zup to his friends—plays quad rugby—a sport for people in wheelchairs. He's a quad rugby champion, winning a gold medal in the 2008 Paralympic Games. "I dream about running all the time," he says, "but you can't live in the past."

Today, Zupan gives talks and raises money for his sport. Anyone who spends time with him forgets that he's in a wheelchair. He lifts weights at the gym every day, drives a car, and goes to music concerts. "A lot of people think quadriplegics can't do anything," he says. To stay in shape, Zupan is careful about his diet and avoids unhealthy and fatty foods. "Just think of me as a human being and an athlete. Because that's who I am."

Bethany Hamilton

Surfer Bethany Hamilton had a dream. She wanted to be a champion in her sport. But in 2003, she lost her left arm when she was attacked by a shark in Hawaii. Three weeks later, she was surfing again. Because she can only use one arm, she has to use her legs more to help her go in the right direction. She's a strong competitive surfer, winning first place in 2005 in the NSSA National Championships. She appears on TV and writes books about her experience.

Hamilton wants to help other people follow their dreams, even when they face great difficulties. "People can do whatever they want if they just set their hearts to it, and just never give up . . . Just go out there and do it," she says.

The 2005 movie *Murderball* made Zupan a star.

Sources: *Gimp*, HarperCollins, 2006 and cnn.com

Hamilton was attacked by a tiger shark in 2003.

A Infer information Complete the paragraph about Mark Zupan. Use <u>can</u>, <u>can't</u>, or <u>has to</u>.

Zupan .... spend most of his time in a wheelchair, but he .... stand up
    1   2
or take a few steps for a short time. He .... go walking or running, but he
                                          3
.... play quad rugby. He .... be careful about his diet so he doesn't get out of
    4   5
shape. He doesn't have complete use of his hands, but he .... lift weights.
                                                            6
He .... drive a car using his feet, but he .... use his hands. A lot of people
    7   8
think quadriplegics .... do anything, but Zupan proves that they ....
                        9   10

B Summarize First, complete the paragraph about Hamilton. Use the simple present tense
or the present continuous. Then on a separate sheet of paper, write a similar paragraph,
summarizing Mark Zupan's routines.

When she surfs, Hamilton .... her legs to help her go in the right direction.
                              1 use
She .... regularly with the world's top woman surfers, and sometimes
        2 compete
she .... In the photo on page 70, she .... next to her
        3 win   4 stand
surfboard, and she .... because she .... again now. Hamilton
                        5 smile   6 surf
.... to help other people with difficult experiences
    7 want
follow their dreams.

> On your *ActiveBook* Self-Study Disc:
> **Extra Reading Comprehension Questions**

NOW YOU CAN Describe someone's routines

A Notepadding Write some notes about your daily routines.

List some things you usually do . . .	List some things you . . .
• in the morning.	• can't do every day. Explain why.
• in the afternoon.	• have to do every day. Explain why.
• in the evening.	• don't have to do every day. Explain why.

B Pair work Interview your partner about
his or her daily routines.

C Group work Now describe your partner's
daily routines to your classmates.

❝ What are some things you
usually do in the morning? ❞

My partner usually gets up at
7:00. But, on Saturdays, she
doesn't have to get up early.

Review

A 🔊 **Listening comprehension** Listen to the conversations.
Check the statements that are true.

1 ☐ He doesn't exercise regularly.
☐ He avoids junk food.
☐ He never watches TV.

2 ☐ She's in great shape.
☐ She hardly ever goes swimming.
☐ She exercises regularly.

3 ☐ He exercises regularly.
☐ He has to be careful about calories.
☐ He can eat everything he wants.

4 ☐ Heeley can't use his legs.
☐ Heeley can't see.
☐ Heeley doesn't need help.

B What activities can you do in these places? Write sentences with <u>can</u>.

an athletic field	I can play . . .
a gym	
a park	

C Choose the best response.

1 "Why don't we go swimming tomorrow?"
a Well, have a great time.
b Sorry, I can't. I have to work.

2 "Why don't we meet at 8:00?"
a Great! When's good for you?
b Sure. Sounds great.

3 "What are you up to?"
a I can't. I have to meet my sister.
b I'm having dinner.

D Answer the questions with real information. Use the simple present
tense or the present continuous in your answer.

1 How often do you go to English class?
(YOU) ....

2 What do you usually do on weekends?
(YOU) ....

3 What are you doing this weekend?
(YOU) ....

3:40/3:41
🎵 *Top Notch Pop*
"A Typical Day"
Lyrics p. 150

E **Writing** On a separate sheet of paper, write an interview in which
someone asks you about your exercise and health habits.

Q: What do you do to stay in shape?

A: Well, I run every morning and I lift weights.

Q: Where do you usually . . . ?

WRITING BOOSTER ▸ p. 142

• *Punctuation of statements and questions*
• *Guidance for Exercise E*

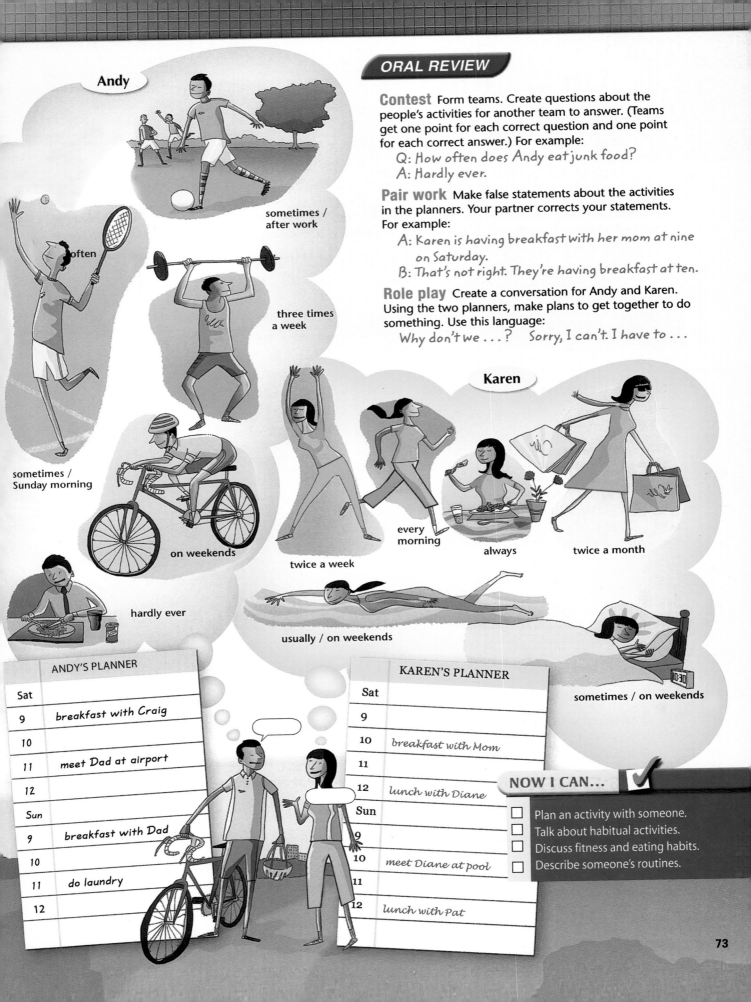

Andy

sometimes /
after work

often

three times
a week

sometimes /
Sunday morning

on weekends

hardly ever

Karen

twice a week

every
morning

always

twice a month

usually / on weekends

sometimes / on weekends

Contest Form teams. Create questions about the people's activities for another team to answer. (Teams get one point for each correct question and one point for each correct answer.) For example:

Q: How often does Andy eat junk food?
A: Hardly ever.

Pair work Make false statements about the activities in the planners. Your partner corrects your statements. For example:

A: Karen is having breakfast with her mom at nine on Saturday.
B: That's not right. They're having breakfast at ten.

Role play Create a conversation for Andy and Karen. Using the two planners, make plans to get together to do something. Use this language:

Why don't we . . . ?   Sorry, I can't. I have to . . .

ANDY'S PLANNER

Sat	
9	breakfast with Craig
10	
11	meet Dad at airport
12	
Sun	
9	breakfast with Dad
10	
11	do laundry
12	

KAREN'S PLANNER

Sat	
9	
10	breakfast with Mom
11	
12	lunch with Diane
Sun	
9	
10	meet Diane at pool
11	
12	lunch with Pat

NOW I CAN... ✔

- ☐ Plan an activity with someone.
- ☐ Talk about habitual activities.
- ☐ Discuss fitness and eating habits.
- ☐ Describe someone's routines.

73

On Vacation

GOALS After Unit 7, you will be able

1 Greet someone arriving from a trip.
2 Ask about someone's vacation.
3 Discuss vacation preferences.
4 Describe good and bad travel experie

TRAVEL SPECIALS *Guaranteed!* Your money refunded if your flight or cruise is canceled.

Tour Europe in 10 days

Fly to London on July 15.

Take pictures at London's Buckingham Palace.

Visit the Eiffel Tower in Paris and ride a boat on the Seine.

Go shopping in Milan. Explore the ruins of the Coliseum in Rome.

Enjoy Vienna's famous desserts. Walk along the old Berlin Wall.

See Copenhagen's Little Mermaid statue.

Fly back home on July 25.

10-night Caribbean Cruise

Leave from Miami on July 15.

Swim in our heated pool … or just lie in the sun all day. Eat in our excellent restaurants. And at night, watch a movie or a show … or go walking!

Go windsurfing in Montego Bay.

Go snorkeling in Cozumel. Explore a beautiful beach in Costa Rica.

Return to Miami on July 25.

A Pair work Complete the chart by writing <u>tour</u> or <u>cruise</u>. Then discuss your answers with a partner.

In your opinion, which travel special would be good for someone who likes . . .		
history? _____	family activities? _____	entertainment? _____
culture? _____	physical activities? _____	good food? _____

B Discussion Which vacation would you like to take? Why?

C 🔊 4:02 **Photo story** Read and listen to a phone call from someone returning from a trip.

Cindy: Hi, Rick. I'm home!
Rick: Cindy! When did you get back?
Cindy: Just yesterday.
Rick: And did you have a good time?
Cindy: I just loved it. I really needed a vacation!

Rick: So, tell me all about your cruise!
Cindy: Well, the people were really great. The food was incredible. And the weather was perfect.
Rick: And what did you do all day?
Cindy: Plenty. In Montego Bay, I went windsurfing. And I had a lot of fun snorkeling in Cozumel.
Rick: Cool!

Cindy: But most of the time I just enjoyed the sun and did absolutely nothing!
Rick: Now that's my kind of vacation!
Cindy: I can't wait for the next one.
Rick: Well, welcome home.

D **Focus on language** Look at the underlined words and expressions in the Photo Story.

1 Find an expression that means "come home."
. . . .

2 Find three words that mean "very good."
. . . .
. . . .
. . . .

E **Think and explain** Complete the statements.

1 When Rick says, "Now that's my kind of vacation!" he means . . . .

2 When Cindy says, "I can't wait for the next one," she means . . . .

F **Discussion** Which part of Cindy's vacation is "your kind of vacation"?

G **Pair work** Complete the questionnaire. Then tell your partner what you usually do on your vacations. Ask about your partner's vacations.

Where do you usually go for vacation?

☐ I stay home.
☐ I visit my family.
☐ I go to the beach.
☐ I go to another city.
☐ I go to another country.
☐ Other _____

75

GOAL | Greet someone arriving from a trip

CONVERSATION MODEL

A 🔊 4:03 Read and listen to someone greeting a person arriving from a trip.

A: Welcome back!

B: Thanks.

A: So, how was the flight?

B: Pretty nice, actually.

A: That's good. Can I give you a hand?

B: That's OK. I'm fine.

A: Are you sure?

B: Absolutely. Thanks!

B 🔊 4:04 **Rhythm and intonation** Listen again and repeat. Then practice the Conversation Model with a partner.

GRAMMAR | *The past tense of be: Review*

I
He   {was
She   wasn't} on time.
It

We   {were
You   weren't} late.
They

Contractions
wasn't = was not
weren't = were not

Questions

Was your flight long? (Yes, it was. / No, it wasn't.)

Were your friends with you? (Yes, they were. / No, they weren't.)

How was the traffic? (It was terrible.)
How long were you away? (Two weeks.)

GRAMMAR BOOSTER ▸ p. 134

• *The past tense of be: form*

A Find the grammar Look at the Photo Story on page 75. Find three examples of the past tense of <u>be</u>.

B Grammar practice Complete the conversations with the affirmative or negative past tense of <u>be</u>.

1 A: Welcome back! How .... the drive?
B: Not great. The traffic .... really awful. There .... so many cars on the road!
A: Too bad. .... you alone?
B: No. My brother .... with me.

2 A: Did you just get in?
B: Yes. My flight .... a little late.
A: .... there a lot of people on the plane?
B: No, there ....

3 A: Where .... you last week?
B: We .... on a cruise.
A: Really? How .... it?
B: It .... pretty short. Only three days!

4 A: So, how .... your parents' trip?
B: Actually, it .... too great.
A: What happened?
B: Their train .... four hours late, so they .... really tired.

Adjectives to describe trips

4:05

A 🔊 Read and listen. Then listen again and repeat.

It was so **comfortable**.

It was quite **scenic**.

It was really **boring**.

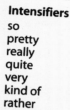

Intensifiers
so
pretty
really
quite
very
kind of
rather

It was kind of **bumpy**.

It was pretty **scary**.

FLIGHT TIME 1 HOUR   FLIGHT TIME 13 HOURS

It was rather **short**. / It was very **long**.

B **Pair work** Use the adjectives and intensifiers in the Vocabulary to describe a trip you took.

"Last year, I went to a small town in the mountains. The bus trip was very bumpy."

Types of trips
a flight   a [bus / train] trip
a drive   a cruise

NOW YOU CAN   Greet someone arriving from a trip

A **Pair work** Greet someone arriving from a trip. Change the Conversation Model, using the adjectives and intensifiers and the past tense of <u>be</u>. Then change roles.

A: Welcome back!

B: ....

A: So, how was the ....?

B: ...., actually.

A: That's .... Can I give you a hand?

B: ....

Don't stop! Ask your partner other questions about the trip:
  Were there a lot of people on the ___ ?
  How long was the ___ ?

Responses
comfortable
scenic   } **That's good!**
short

boring
bumpy
scary   } **That's too bad!**
long

B **Change partners** Greet someone arriving from another type of trip. Use other adjectives from the Vocabulary. Ask more questions.

GOAL   **Ask about someone's vacation**

GRAMMAR   *The simple past tense: Review*

I
She   } arrived at three.
It   } didn't arrive until six.
They

Did he **have** a good time? (Yes, he did.)
Did they **cancel** your flight? (No, they didn't.)

Where **did** you **go**? (We went to Italy.)
When **did** they **get back**? (On Tuesday.)
What **did** she **do** every day? (She visited museums.)
How many countries **did** you **see**? (Three.)

Regular verbs: spelling

+ ed	+ d	+ ied
visited	arrived	study → studied
watched	changed	try → tried
played	liked	

4:06
🔊 **Some irregular verbs**

buy	**bought**	find	**found**	leave	**left**	sleep	**slept**
come	**came**	fly	**flew**	lose	**lost**	spend	**spent**
do	**did**	get	**got**	meet	**met**	steal	**stole**
drink	**drank**	go	**went**	ride	**rode**	swim	**swam**
eat	**ate**	have	**had**	see	**saw**	take	**took**

See page 122 for a more complete list.

GRAMMAR BOOSTER ▸ p. 135
• The simple past tense: more on spelling, usage, and form

A Find the grammar Look at the Photo Story on page 75.
Circle all the verbs in the simple past tense. Which are irregular verbs?

B Grammar practice Complete Joan's postcard with past forms of the verbs.

Dear Angela,

We're here! The flight _____ nice, and it
                                    1 be
_____ too long. I _____ the whole time.
2 not / be   3 sleep
Yesterday, we _____ swimming. We
                        4 go
_____ fresh seafood and _____ coconut
5 eat   6 drink
milk from coconuts right off the trees. In the evening, we

_____ a wonderful dinner. The service _____
7 have   8 be
great, and the waiters _____ really nice. After the
                          9 be
meal, a pop band _____ , and we
                      10 play
_____ some very nice people at the next table.
11 meet
We _____ until after midnight. We
      12 not / leave
_____ such a good time! This morning,
13 have
we _____ into town and _____ postcards.
      14 walk   15 buy
More later!

                                        Joan

Angela Meyer

55 White Street

Belleville, NY 10514

USA

C Pair work Write five questions about Joan's vacation, using the simple past tense.
Then practice asking and answering your questions with a partner.

Example:

What did she do on the flight?   2 ....   4 ....

1 ....   3 ....   5 ....

D Grammar practice Imagine that you just got back from one of the vacations on page 74. On a separate sheet of paper, write at least five sentences describing what you did, using the simple past tense.

We left Miami on July 15. ...

CONVERSATION MODEL

4:08

A 🔊 Read and listen to someone describing a vacation.

A: Were you on vacation?

B: Yes, I was. I went to Paris.

A: No kidding! Did you have a good time?

B: Fantastic. I stayed in a really nice hotel and ate at some wonderful restaurants.

A: That sounds nice. Tell me more.

4:09

B 🔊 **Rhythm and intonation** Listen again and repeat. Then practice the Conversation Model with a partner.

NOW YOU CAN   **Ask about someone's vacation**

A Pair work Change the Conversation Model, using the vacation ads and positive adjectives. Then change roles.

A: Were you on vacation?

B: Yes, I was. I ....

A: ....! Did you have a good time?

B: .... I .... and ....

A: That sounds .... Tell me more.

Positive adjectives	
incredible	terrific
fantastic	wonderful
great	perfect

Don't stop! Ask and answer more questions, using the simple past tense.
Did you ___ ?   Where ___ ?
What ___ ?   When ___ ?

B Change partners Practice the conversation again about a different vacation.

PERTH, AUSTRALIA
GO SURFING
PLAY ON THE BEACH ALL DAY

COME TO EGYPT
RIDE A CAMEL
VISIT THE GREAT PYRAMIDS

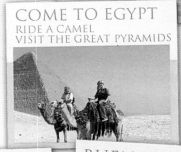

VISIT NEW YORK!
GO SHOPPING
SEE A BROADWAY PLAY

BUENOS AIRES, ARGENTINA!
EAT A DELICIOUS STEAK

BEFORE YOU READ

A 4:10 🔊 **Vocabulary** • *Adjectives for vacations* Read and listen. Then listen again and repeat.

Also remember:
boring   fantastic
cool   scenic

It was **relaxing**.   It was **exciting**.   It was **interesting**.   It was **unusual**.

B Pair work Use the Vocabulary to describe one of your vacations.

> " Last year, I went to the beach. It was so relaxing. "

READING 4:11 🔊

World Traveler *Did you have a good time?*

Our readers share their experiences on our most popular vacation packages.

ADVENTURE IN CHILE

Go skiing and snowboarding in Valle Nevado
Just 60 kilometers / 37 miles from Santiago

"We just got back! There was nothing but sun and snow, but there was plenty to do. We went jogging every night in a terrific park . We swam every day in a heated pool and worked out in an incredible gym. The shopping was terrific! And there were so many great restaurants to choose from. Oh, and I almost forgot . . . the views of the Andes Mountains were amazing!"

—Alison Nack, Montreal, Canada

TAKE IT EASY IN THAILAND

Enjoy some of the world's top spas
Luxury and service at prices you can afford

"Back home, we work very hard, and we really needed a vacation. The staff at the spa knew just how to take care of us. My wife and I got wonderful massages and other spa treatments. They even put hot rocks on our backs! We enjoyed excellent healthy meals every day. We loved our spa vacation in Thailand. It was really hard to come back home!"

—Kenji Watanabe, Nagoya, Japan

Global Village Project

Learn about another culture and help the world
No experience necessary

"My vacation in Tajikistan lasted twenty-six days, and we helped to build new homes for ten of those days. The other days we went sightseeing and bought souvenirs. The people were incredibly nice, and I loved the food. There were twelve other volunteers on this trip. The work was actually fun, and we got to know each other really well. In the end we felt really good. I'd definitely do it again!"

—Arturo Manuel Reyes, Monterrey, Mexico

Sources: skitotal.com; spastay.com; habitat.org

A **Activate language from a text** Find the expressions below in the Reading.
Then use them to talk about a vacation you took.

> • "There was plenty to do."
> • "It was really hard to come back home."
> • "I'd definitely do it again."

> 66 In 2004 I went on a cruise. There was
> plenty to do. I went swimming and . . . 99

B **Draw conclusions** Choose a vacation package from page 80 for each person.
Explain your reasons.

66 I love to meet new people and learn how to do new things. 99

66 I love sports. I always like to do something new and exciting. 99

66 I like to go to places where other people don't go—off the beaten path. 99

66 I need a vacation where I don't have to do <u>anything</u>. 99

C **Identify supporting details** Now choose one of the vacations for yourself. Explain why you chose it. Use the Vocabulary on page 80.

> On your *ActiveBook* Self-Study Disc:
> **Extra Reading Comprehension Questions**

NOW YOU CAN Discuss vacation preferences

A **Frame your ideas** Complete the questionnaire. Then compare answers with a partner.

Need a Vacation? Check all your preferences:

How often do you go on vacation? ☐ never   ☐ once or twice a year   ☐ more than twice a year

I prefer vacations that are . . .

☐ relaxing
☐ exciting
☐ interesting
☐ unusual
☐ inexpensive
☐ scenic
☐ other _____

I like vacations with . . .

☐ lots of history and culture
☐ nature and wildlife
☐ sports and physical activities
☐ family activities
☐ great entertainment
☐ people who speak my language

☐ top-notch hotels
☐ great food
☐ warm weather
☐ beautiful beaches
☐ friendly people
☐ other _____
_____
_____

Do you need a vacation right now? ☐ Not really.   ☐ Maybe.   ☐ You bet I do!

B **Discussion** Now discuss your vacation preferences. Tell your classmates what's important to you.

> 66 For me, warm weather and great
> entertainment are pretty important. 99

GOAL **Describe good and bad travel experiences**

A 🔊 4:12 **Vocabulary** • *Bad and good travel experiences* Read and listen. Then listen again and repeat.

Bad experiences

The weather was { **horrible.** **awful.** **pretty bad.** **terrible.**

The people were { **unfriendly.** **cold.**

They lost my luggage.

Someone stole my wallet.

Good experiences

The weather was { **amazing.** **fantastic.** **terrific.** **wonderful.**

The people were { **friendly.** **warm.**

They found my luggage.

Someone returned my wallet.

B Look at the pictures. Complete the sentences.

1 ..Someone.stole.. my purse. **2** The food .... **3** The waiters ....

4 The entertainment .... **5** .... my luggage.

A 🔊 **Listen for main ideas** Listen to the conversations. Check whether, at the end of the vacation, the person had a good experience or a bad one.

4:13

1 ☐ a good experience   ☐ a bad experience   **3** ☐ a good experience   ☐ a bad experience

2 ☐ a good experience   ☐ a bad experience   **4** ☐ a good experience   ☐ a bad experience

B 🔊 **Listen for details** Listen again and complete the statements about each vacation.

4:14

1 The food was really (good / bad).
The room was (great / terrible).
The entertainment was really (good / bad).

2 The hotel was (terrible / terrific).
Someone stole their (luggage / car).
Disney World was (horrible / wonderful).

3 He didn't have any more (clothes / money).
The people were very (nice / cold).
The hotel was (great / terrible).
Someone stole his (passport / laptop).

4 The food was (great / awful).
The people were (cold / nice).
The vacation was too (short / long).

NOW YOU CAN   Describe good and bad travel experiences

A Notepadding Make a list of some of your good and bad travel experiences.

Good experiences	Bad experiences
I went to Bangkok, and the people were really friendly.	When I went to Los Angeles, they lost my luggage.

Good experiences	Bad experiences

Ideas
- the trip
- the weather
- the food
- the service
- the hotels
- the people
- the activities
- your luggage

B Pair work Now tell your partner about the good and bad travel experiences you listed. Ask questions about your partner's experiences.

♻️ **Be sure to recycle this language.**

Ask
How was the ___ ?
What did you ___ ?
When did you ___ ?
How many ___ did you ___ ?
Tell me about ___ .

Respond
That's good.
That's great!
No kidding!
Oh, no!
That's too bad.
I'm sorry to hear that.

Describe
I had a ___ time.
The [flight] was ___ .
The ___ drove me crazy.
The ___ didn't work.
I was in the mood for ___ , but ___ .
They didn't accept credit cards.

Review

More Practice

ActiveBook *Self-Study Disc*

grammar · vocabulary · listening
reading · speaking · pronunciation

A 🔊 4:15 **Listening comprehension** Listen to each person describing a travel experience. Write the number of the speaker in the box for the type of trip he or she took.

☐ a drive   ☐ a train trip   ☐ a flight   ☐ a beach vacation

B 🔊 4:16 Listen again. Circle the adjective that best describes each experience.

1 Her trip was very (short / scary / scenic).

2 His trip was quite (scary / unusual / relaxing).

3 Her trip was pretty (short / scary / boring).

4 His trip was really (short / scenic / boring).

C Complete each conversation with a question in the simple past tense.

1 A: .... on vacation?
   B: We went to Greece.

2 A: .... stay there?
   B: Two weeks.

3 A: .... every day?
   B: We walked along the beach and enjoyed the sun.

4 A: .... get back home?
   B: Last night.

D Complete each statement or question about vacations. Use the past tense form.

1 (we / buy) .... a lot of fantastic things on our vacation.

2 (where / you / eat) .... dinner last night?

3 (we / sleep) .... right on the beach. (it / be) .... so relaxing.

4 (my sister / get back) .... last weekend. (she / have) .... an amazing time.

5 (my friend / eat) .... some rather good food on her trip to Hong Kong.

6 (when / she / arrive) .... at the hotel?

7 (I / have) .... a terrible time. (the people / be) .... quite unfriendly.

8 (we / see) .... an interesting play in London. And (it / be) .... pretty inexpensive.

9 (my wife and I / go running) .... every morning on the beach during our vacation.

10 (my brother / meet) .... some unusual people on his trip.

E **Writing** On a separate sheet of paper, write about a vacation you took. Answer these questions.

- Where did you go?
- How was the travel?
- How was the weather?
- What did you do?
- Did you have a good time?

WRITING BOOSTER ▸ p. 145

- *Time order*
- *Guidance for Exercise E*

4:17/4:18
🎵 *Top Notch Pop*
"My Dream Vacation"
Lyrics p. 150

In 2010, I went on a great trip to . . .

Contest Form two teams. Each team takes turns making a statement about the vacation, using the simple past tense. Continue until one team cannot say anything more. (Each team has thirty seconds to make a statement.)

Role play Create a conversation for the two women on February 5. Start like this:

Were you on vacation?

Pair work Choose one of the vacation pictures. Create a conversation. Start with one of these, or your own idea:
- Can I give you a hand?
- Excuse me!
- This bed is terrible!
- This is so relaxing.

January 15

January 17-22

ARRIVALS

February 5

NOW I CAN...
- ☐ Greet someone arriving from a trip.
- ☐ Ask about someone's vacation.
- ☐ Discuss vacation preferences.
- ☐ Describe good and bad travel experiences.

Shopping for Clothes

GOALS After Unit 8, you will be abl

1 Shop and pay for clothes.
2 Ask for a different size or color.
3 Navigate a mall or department store.
4 Discuss clothing do's and don'ts.

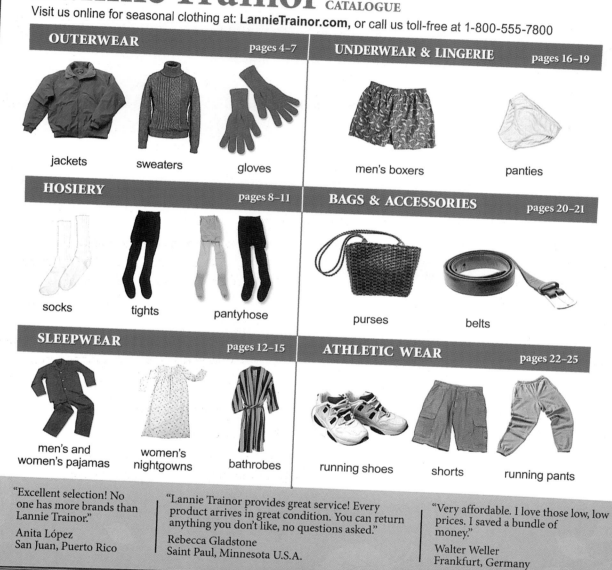

Lannie Trainor CATALOGUE

Visit us online for seasonal clothing at: **LannieTrainor.com,** or call us toll-free at **1-800-555-7800**

OUTERWEAR   pages 4–7

jackets   sweaters   gloves

UNDERWEAR & LINGERIE   pages 16–19

men's boxers   panties

HOSIERY   pages 8–11

socks   tights   pantyhose

BAGS & ACCESSORIES   pages 20–21

purses   belts

SLEEPWEAR   pages 12–15

men's and women's pajamas   women's nightgowns   bathrobes

ATHLETIC WEAR   pages 22–25

running shoes   shorts   running pants

"Excellent selection! No one has more brands than Lannie Trainor."

Anita López
San Juan, Puerto Rico

"Lannie Trainor provides great service! Every product arrives in great condition. You can return anything you don't like, no questions asked."

Rebecca Gladstone
Saint Paul, Minnesota U.S.A.

"Very affordable. I love those low, low prices. I saved a bundle of money."

Walter Weller
Frankfurt, Germany

A 🔊 4:19 **Vocabulary** • *Clothing departments* Listen and repeat.

B Discussion What clothes are good to buy from a catalogue? What do you like to buy from a store? Why?

❝I like to buy running shoes from a store because I want to be sure the size is right.❞

C 🔊 4:20 **Photo story** Read and listen to a conversation between a clerk and a customer about a sweater the customer wants to buy.

ENGLISH FOR TODAY'S WORLD
connecting people from different cultures
and language backgrounds

Shopper: Excuse me. How much is that V-neck?
Clerk: This red one? It's $55.
Shopper: That's not too bad. And it's really nice.

Shopper: Could I get it in a larger size?
Clerk: Here you go. This one's a medium. Would you like to try it on?

Shopper: No, thanks. I'll just take it. It's a present for my sister. Would you be nice enough to gift wrap it for me?
Clerk: Of course!

Shopper: Chinese speaker; Clerk: Russian speaker

D **Think and explain** Complete each statement. Then explain your answer.

1 The shopper wants to know the ...... of the sweater.
   a price   **b** size
   How do you know? She says,
   " How much is that V-neck? .... "

2 She asks the clerk for ....
   a another color   **b** another size
   How do you know? The shopper says,
   " .... "

3 The clerk brings the shopper a ....
   a different size   **b** different color
   How do you know? The clerk says,
   " .... "

4 The sweater is ....
   a for the shopper   **b** for a different person
   How do you know? The shopper says,
   " .... "

E **Focus on language** Complete each statement with a quotation from the Photo Story.

1 The shopper says, "................................." to get the clerk's attention.
2 The shopper says, " ...." to say that the price of the sweater is OK.
3 The clerk says, "................................." when she gives the shopper the second sweater.

F **Personalize** What's important to you when you shop for clothes? Complete the chart.

	Not important	Important	Very important
Prices	○	○	○
Brands	○	○	○
Selection	○	○	○
Service	○	○	○

G **Discussion** Compare charts with your classmates. Explain your reasons.

GOAL Shop and pay for clothes

VOCABULARY *Types of clothing and shoes*

4:21
🔊 Read and listen. Then listen again and repeat.

casual clothes	sweaters and jackets	shoes
① jeans ② a T-shirt	① a crewneck ② a cardigan	① oxfords ② loafers
③ a sweatshirt ④ a polo shirt	③ a turtleneck ④ a V-neck	③ sandals ④ running shoes
⑤ sweatpants	⑤ a windbreaker ⑥ a blazer	⑤ pumps ⑥ flats

GRAMMAR *Uses of object pronouns*

Subject pronouns		Object pronouns
I	→	me
you	→	you
he	→	him
she	→	her
it	→	it
we	→	us
they	→	them

As direct objects

direct object (noun)		direct object (pronoun)
I want **the cardigan**.	→	I want it.
I love **these pumps**.	→	I love them.

In prepositional phrases

prepositional phrase (with nouns)		prepositional phrase (with pronouns)
We gave the V-neck **to Jane**.	→	We gave the V-neck to her.
He's buying a blazer **for his wife**.	→	He's buying a blazer for her.

In a sentence with both a direct object and a prepositional phrase, the direct object comes first.

We gave the hat to Jane. NOT We gave

He's buying it for her. NOT He's buying

GRAMMAR BOOSTER ▸ p. 136

• *Direct and indirect objects: usage*

A Grammar practice First, underline the direct object in each sentence. Then complete each conversation, replacing the direct object noun or noun phrase with an object pronoun.

1 A: Did you buy <u>the green sweatpants</u>?
B: Yes, I bought ..*them*...

2 A: Don't you love these cool windbreakers?
B: Yes, I really love ....

3 A: Should I buy this crewneck over here?
B: No, don't buy ....

4 A: Did you see the blue polo shirts?
B: Yes, I saw .... on that rack.

5 A: Does your daughter want this cardigan?
B: Yes, she wants ....

6 A: Who did she give the old jacket to?
B: She gave .... to me.

B Grammar practice Unscramble the words and phrases to write statements.

1 I / it / for her / am buying ....

2 they / them / for us / are getting ....

3 please / it / to me / give ....

4 for my son-in-law / I / them / need ....

5 it / he / is / finding / for me ....

CONVERSATION MODEL

4:22

A 🔊 Read and listen to a conversation in which someone is paying for clothes.

A: I'll take these polo shirts, please.

B: Certainly. How would you like to pay for them?

A: Excuse me?

B: Cash or charge?

A: Charge, please. And could you gift wrap them for me?

B: Absolutely.

4:23

B 🔊 **Rhythm and intonation** Listen again and repeat. Then practice the Conversation Model with a partner.

C Find the grammar Find and circle all the object pronouns in the Conversation Model.

NOW YOU CAN Shop and pay for clothes

A Look at the Vocabulary on page 88, and look back at the clothing catalogue on page 86. Choose three items of clothing you'd like to buy for yourself or as gifts.

B Pair work Change the Conversation Model to buy one of the things you chose. Use the correct object pronouns. Then change roles.

A: I'll take ...., please.

B: .... How would you like to pay for ....?

A: Excuse me?

B: Cash or charge?

A: ...., please. And could you gift wrap .... for me?

B: ....

Don't stop!
Before you pay, ask about other clothing.

C Change partners Create another conversation. Use different articles of clothing.

VOCABULARY   *Clothing that comes in "pairs"*

A 🔊 4:24 Read and listen. Then listen again and repeat.

(a pair of) **gloves**

(a pair of) **pantyhose**

(a pair of) **tights**

(a pair of) **panties**

(a pair of) **pajamas**

(a pair of) **shorts**

(a pair of) **pants**

(a pair of) **boxers**

(a pair of) **briefs**

(a pair of) **socks**

B 🔊 4:25 **Listening comprehension** Listen to the conversations. Infer the department each shopper should go to.

1 She should go to ....

2 She should go to ....

3 She got them in ....

4 They're in ....

Departments
Men's underwear
Athletic wear
Outerwear
Lingerie
Sleepwear
Hosiery

GRAMMAR   *Comparative adjectives*

Use comparative adjectives to compare two people, places, things, or ideas.

Do you have these pants in a larger size? This pair is a little tight.
I need shoes that are more comfortable. These are very small.
Do you have a pair of less expensive gloves? These are just too expensive.

Use <u>than</u> after the adjective when you compare two items.

That suit is nicer than the one I'm wearing.
These gloves are more expensive than the other ones.

+ <u>er</u>	+ <u>r</u>	+ <u>ier</u>	consonant + <u>er</u>
small → smaller	large → larger	heavy → heavier	big → bigger
cheap → cheaper	loose → looser	pretty → prettier	hot → hotter

Irregular forms	
good →	better
bad →	worse

BUT use <u>more</u> or <u>less</u> with adjectives that have two or more syllables and don't end in –y.

more expensive / less comfortable

GRAMMAR BOOSTER ▸ p. 137
• *Comparative adjectives: spelling rules*

A Grammar practice Write the opposite of each comparative adjective.

1 smaller ...larger....
2 taller ....
3 lighter ....
4 tighter ....
5 more expensive ....
6 less popular ....

B Complete each conversation with comparative adjectives. Use <u>than</u> if necessary.

1 A: I just love these pajamas, but I wish they were ....
   (warm)
   B: What about these? Blue is a really flattering color for you, and they're much ....
   (expensive)

2 A: Don't take that nightgown to Hawaii! It's .... it is here. Take something ....
   (hot)   (light)
   B: Good idea.

3 A: What do you think of these red gloves?
   B: Beautiful. They're .... the black ones. And they're ...., too.
   (pretty)   (cheap)

4 A: Excuse me. Do these pants come in a .... length?
   (long)
   B: I'm sure they do. Let me see if I can find you something ....
   (good)

CONVERSATION MODEL

A 4:26 Read and listen to someone asking for a different size.

A: Excuse me. Do you have these gloves in a smaller size? I need a medium.

B: Yes, we do. Here you go.

A: Thanks.

B: Would you like to take them?

A: Yes, please. Thanks for your help.

B: My pleasure.

Sizes
S   small
M   medium
L   large
XL   extra large
XXL   extra extra large

B 4:27 **Rhythm and intonation** Listen again and repeat. Then practice the Conversation Model with a partner.

NOW YOU CAN | Ask for a different size or color

A Notepadding On the notepad, make a list of clothes you'd like to buy.

I'd like to buy:

B Pair work Change the Conversation Model. Use comparatives and your list of clothes. Ask for a different size or color. Then change roles.

A: Excuse me. Do you have .... in ....?

B: Yes, we do. Here you go.

A: Thanks.

B: Would you like to take ....?

A: .... Thanks for your help.

B: ....

Don't stop!
• Ask to see other clothes.
• Pay for the clothes.

Ideas
in a smaller size
in a larger size
in a darker / lighter color
in [black, white, etc.]
in size [10, 34, etc.]

C Change partners Ask about other types of clothes.

GOAL Navigate a mall or department store

4:28

🔊 **Vocabulary** • *Interior locations and directions* Read and listen. Then listen again and repeat.

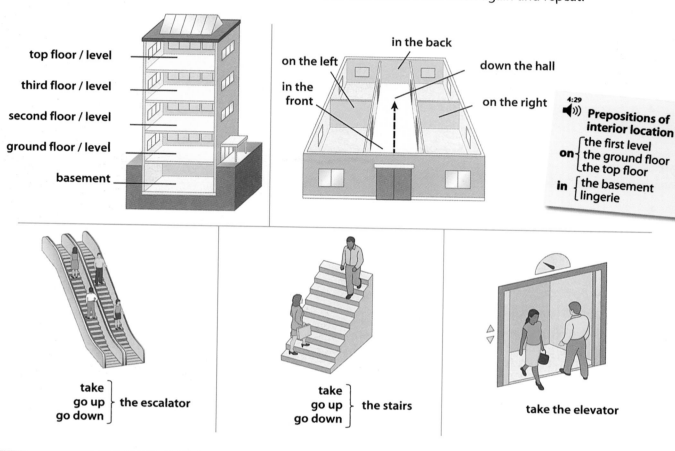

4:30

A 🔊 **Understand locations and directions** Listen to directions in a department store. Write the number of each location in the white boxes on the floor diagrams.

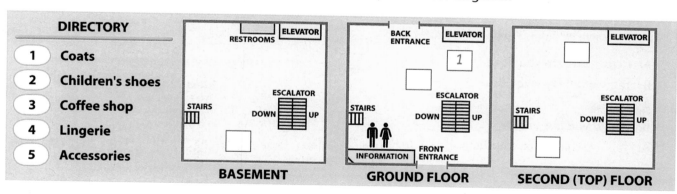

B Pair work Take turns asking for and giving directions to any of the locations.

Contrastive stress for clarification

A 🔊 **4:31** Read and listen. Then listen again and repeat.

> **A:** The shoe department is upstairs, on the **third floor**.
>
> **B:** Excuse me? The **first floor**?
>
> **A:** No. It's on the **third floor**.

B **Pair work** Now practice the conversation with a partner.

NOW YOU CAN Navigate a mall or department store

A **Notepadding** Choose five departments from the store directory and write one thing you'd like to get in each department.

Department	I'd like . . .
Men's Outerwear	a jacket

Department	I'd like . . .

B **Wordposting** Put the four categories below on a separate sheet of paper. With a partner, make a list of language you know for each category.

1 Ask for directions
2 Give directions and state locations
3 Ask for a size, color, etc.
4 Pay for things

1	Ask for directions
	I'm looking for the hosiery department.

C **Role play** Navigate the department store, using the floor plan. Create a conversation between the shopper and the person at the information desk. Use your notepad and your wordposts. Then change partners, roles, and items.

> 66 Excuse me. I'm looking for . . . 99

STORE DIRECTORY

Bags and Accessories	Ground Floor
Electronics	Basement
Hosiery	Ground Floor
Lingerie	Ground Floor
Men's Athletic Wear	2
Men's Casual	2
Men's Outerwear	2
Men's Shoes	2
Men's Sleepwear	2
Men's Underwear	2
Photo Studio	Basement
Restaurant	Basement
Small Appliances	Basement
Women's Casual	Ground Floor
Women's Shoes	Ground Floor

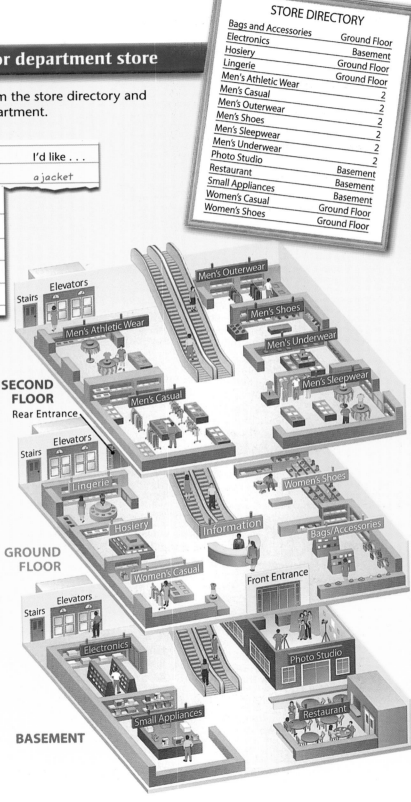

BEFORE YOU READ

 4:32

Vocabulary • *Formality and appropriateness* Read and listen to each pair of antonyms. Then listen again and repeat.

Formality	Appropriateness	Strictness
formal for special events when casual clothes are not OK	**appropriate** socially correct	**liberal** without many rules for appropriate dress
informal for everyday events when casual clothes are OK	**inappropriate** socially incorrect	**conservative** with more rules for appropriate dress

READING 4:33 ◀))

The Savvy Voyager   go   new   search   reply   login   join

Travelin'Girl

Hello! Traveling to Dar es Salaam, Tanzania next week and I need some info on clothing do's and don'ts. I'm in Holland right now where the dress code is pretty liberal, more liberal than where I come from in Germany. The attitude is "anything goes," and they wear some pretty wild things here! How strict are the "rules" there?

Jillian25

Hi, Travelin'Girl,
I go there quite a bit, and my general rule of thumb for East Africa is to keep your shoulders covered and to wear below-the-knee pants or skirts—no sleeveless shirts or tank tops. The culture is pretty conservative, and women dress modestly. Don't show too much skin.

TallPaul

OK, Jillian25. But it's incredibly hot and humid there, just about all year round. Travelin'Girl should pack for the heat: cotton blouses (in light colors); casual, comfortable, light pants; sandals. She didn't say—is this a business trip or pleasure?

Travelin'Girl

A mix of both—a little business in Dar (with my husband), then a quick safari to see the animals. Then I plan on spending at least one weekend at the beach. What's the story there?

Jillian25

There really are no hard and fast rules, but in tourist areas like beaches, it's more informal and relaxed, and most modest clothing is OK. A bathing suit's fine at the beach, as long as it's not too revealing. But in general, in towns near the coast, the rules are stricter and it's inappropriate to wear shorts or miniskirts, so carry a piece of cotton cloth that you can fix easily around your waist.

TallPaul

And let's not forget your husband. For business and formal meetings, a lightweight suit is always appropriate for both of you (and a tie for him).

Tanzanian woman in modest dress

A Paraphrase Explain in your own words what clothing is appropriate in Tanzania, according to the blog.

B Identify supporting details Check <u>true</u>, <u>false</u>, or <u>no info</u>. Explain the reason why you chose each answer.

	true	false	no info
1 "Jillian25" says she is a travel agent.	☐	☐	☐
2 "Travelin'Girl" wants to dress appropriately in Tanzania.	☐	☐	☐
3 "Travelin'Girl" is traveling alone.	☐	☐	☐
4 Dar is in East Africa.	☐	☐	☐
5 "Travelin'Girl" and her husband have children.	☐	☐	☐
6 Women are expected to dress conservatively in Tanzania.	☐	☐	☐

C Apply information Imagine you are going on the same trip as "Travelin'Girl." Plan your clothes for a one-week visit to Tanzania. Be specific. Explain your choices.

> ❝I think I'll take three pairs of shorts because this is a vacation and I plan to spend most of my time at the beach . . .❞

On your *ActiveBook* Self-Study Disc:
Extra Reading Comprehension Questions

NOW YOU CAN | **Discuss clothing do's and don'ts**

A Frame your ideas Take the opinion survey.

WHAT'S YOUR PERSONAL DRESS CODE?

Check <u>agree</u> or <u>disagree</u>.	agree	disagree
It's OK for men to wear shorts on the street.	☐	☐
It's OK for women to wear shorts on the street.	☐	☐
It's OK to wear sandals in an office.	☐	☐
It's important for men to wear ties in an office.	☐	☐
It's OK for men to wear sleeveless T-shirts in a restaurant.	☐	☐
It's OK for women to wear revealing clothes in a religious institution.	☐	☐

HOW WOULD YOU RATE YOURSELF?

☐ CONSERVATIVE   ☐ LIBERAL   ☐ "ANYTHING GOES!"

B Notepadding With a partner, write some clothing do's and don'ts for visitors to your country. Do the same rules apply to both men and women? Use the survey as a guide.

in offices and formal restaurants:

in casual social settings:

in religious institutions:

C Group work Now discuss clothing do's and don'ts for your country. Does everyone agree?

Text-mining (optional)
Underline language in the Reading on page 94 to use in the Group Work. For example:
"My general rule of thumb is . . ."

Review

A 🔊 4:34 **Listening comprehension** Listen to the conversations. Use the context to infer which department the people are in. Listen more than once if necessary.

1 ....
2 ....
3 ....
4 ....
5 ....

Departments
Shoes
Bags and Accessories
Hosiery
Outerwear
Sleepwear
Lingerie
Electronics

B Complete the chart with the appropriate kinds of shoes and clothes for certain places and occasions.

	Shoes	Clothes
To class or work		
To formal occasions		
On the weekend		

C Complete the travel article with the comparative form of each adjective. Use **than** when necessary.

When you travel, think carefully about the clothes you pack. As far as color is concerned, ...
1 dark
colors are usually ....
2 practical
. For ....
3 cool
destinations, a blazer can be ....
4 convenient
a windbreaker or cardigan because you can wear it in ....
5 conservative
settings such as offices and ....
6 formal
restaurants. For travel to ....
7 hot
areas of the world, ...
8 light
clothes are ....
9 comfortable
....
10 heavy
ones.

4:35/4:36
Top Notch Pop
"Anything Goes"
Lyrics p. 150

D Rewrite each sentence. Change the direct and indirect object nouns and noun phrases to object pronouns.

1 Please show the loafers to my husband. .....*Please show them to him.*..........................

2 They sent the jeans to their grandchildren. ....

3 How is she paying Robert for the clothes? ....

4 When are we buying the gift for Marie? ....

E **Writing** Imagine that you have a friend from another country who is coming to visit you. Write a letter or e-mail to your friend, explaining what to pack for the trip. Give your friend advice on appropriate and inappropriate dress.

WRITING BOOSTER ▸ p. 146
• *Connecting ideas with* because *and* since
• *Guidance for Exercise E*

Hi! Here are some clothing tips for your visit. First of all, the "rules" here are...

Taking Transportation

GOALS | After Unit 9, you will be able

1 Discuss schedules and buy tickets.
2 Book travel services.
3 Understand airport announcements.
4 Describe transportation problems.

Buses from Lima to Nazca

DESTINATION	FREQUENCY	DEPARTURE	ARRIVAL	STOPS	BUS TERMINAL
Lima - Nazca	Daily	04:30	10:45	Paracas	Terminal Nazca
Lima - Nazca	Daily	07:00	13:30	Paracas-Ica	Terminal Nazca
Lima - Nazca	Daily	13:30	20:00	Paracas-Ica	Terminal Nazca
Lima - Nazca	Daily	14:00	20:00	Non-stop	Terminal Nazca
Lima - Nazca	Daily	17:30	23:30	Non-stop	Terminal Nazca

BEIJING to SHANGHAI

Train No.	Depart (BEIJING)	Arrive (SHANGHAI)	Travel Time	Air-conditioned
D31	11:05	20:49	0d 09h 44m	Yes
1461	14:42	12:49	0d 22h 07m	No
Z21	19:32	07:00	0d 11h 28m	Yes
Z13	19:38	07:06	0d 11h 28m	Yes
Z7	19:44	07:12	0d 11h 28m	Yes

CATICLAN to MANILA

Flight No.	Departure	Arrival	Frequency	Aircraft Type
2P 036	0705	0815	DAILY	DH3
2P 038	0725	0835	DAILY	DH3
2P 040	0805	0915	DAILY	DH3
2P 046	1040	1150	DAILY	DH3
2P 048	1700	1810	DAILY	DH3

Sources: mysteryperu.com; travelchinaguide.com; airphils.com

A Use the schedules to find the answers to the questions.

1 It's now 10:00 A.M. When is the next bus to Nazca?

2 And when is the next non-stop bus to Nazca?

3 How much time does it take to get from Beijing to Shanghai on train 1461?

4 Which train is faster, train 1461 or train D31?

5 What time does flight 2P 046 depart for Manila? When does it arrive?

B Pair work Ask your partner more questions about each schedule.

C 🔊 **Photo story** Read and listen to a conversation between two people trying to catch a flight.

Marcos: Excuse me. Do you speak English?

Roger: Actually I'm French. But, yes.

Marcos: Thank goodness! I'm looking for Terminal 2.

Roger: No problem. That's where I'm going. Just follow me.

Roger: So where are you flying today?

Marcos: Manila. Then I'm connecting to a flight home.

Roger: Well, that's a coincidence. I'm on my way to Manila, too. Flight 56?

Marcos: Yes. But we should hurry. It's boarding in fifteen minutes.

Roger: And where is home?

Marcos: Brazil. São Paulo.

Roger: No kidding! I'm going to go to São Paulo next week!

Marcos: Really? What a small world!

Marcos: Portuguese speaker; Roger: French speaker

D **Focus on language** Find an underlined phrase or sentence in the Photo Story that has the same meaning as:

1 I'm traveling to …　　**2** Let's walk faster.　　**3** I'm changing to …

E **Think and explain** Circle T (true), F (false), or NI (no information). Then explain each answer.

T　F　NI　**1**　Flight 56 leaves from Terminal 2.　　T　F　NI　**4**　Marcos is staying in Manila.

T　F　NI　**2**　Roger lives in France.　　T　F　NI　**5**　Roger is staying in Manila.

T　F　NI　**3**　Roger and Marcos are both flying to Manila.　　T　F　NI　**6**　The two men catch the flight.

F **Pair work** Complete the chart with the means of transportation you prefer for each occasion. Then discuss your choices with a partner.

To school or work	bus	affordable, convenient, I can read or work.

	Means of transportation	Reason
To school or work		
To social events on weekends		
For vacations in my country		
For vacations outside of my country		

♻ **Be sure to recycle this language.**

popular	cheap
convenient	scenic
affordable	boring
comfortable	long
expensive	short
relaxing	scary

VOCABULARY *Kinds of tickets and trips*

A 🔊 5:03 Read and listen. Then listen again and repeat.

a one-way ticket

a round-trip ticket

JAPAN RAIL	Kodama (local)	Nozomi (express)
Tokyo	10:13	10:20
Odawara	10:30	—
Atami	11:00	—
Maibara	13:39	—
Kyoto	14:04	12:38

the local   the express

a direct flight

a non-stop flight

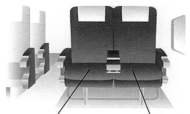

an aisle seat   a window seat

B Complete the conversations with words and phrases from the Vocabulary.

1 A: Would you like a window or an aisle?

B: .... I like to walk around.

2 A: Is Flight 3 a .... flight?

B: No. It's a .... flight. It makes a stop, but you don't have to change planes.

3 A: Do you want a .... ticket to Rome?

B: Actually, I need a .... I'm not coming back!

4 A: I'm sorry. It's too late to make the ....

B: Well, I'll take .... I'm not in a hurry.

GRAMMAR *Modals should and could*

should

Use should and the base form of a verb to give advice.

You **shouldn't take** that flight. You **should take** the non-stop.
Should they **take** the bus? (Yes, they **should**. / No, they **shouldn't**.)
When **should** we **leave**? (Before 2:00.)

could

Use could and the base form of a verb to suggest or ask about alternatives or possibilities.

The express bus is full, but you **could take** the local.
Could I **take** the 2:20? (Yes, you **could**. / No, you **couldn't**.)

GRAMMAR BOOSTER ▸ p. 138

- *Modals: form and meaning*
- *Common errors*

A Grammar practice Complete each statement or question with **should** or **could** and the base form.

1 .... the express. The local arrives too late.
    He / take

2 They said .... two aisle seats or an aisle and a window.
    we / have

3 .... a round-trip ticket. That way you won't have to wait in line twice.

You / get

4 Which train ....? We absolutely have to be there on time.

we / take

5 .... a ticket at the station or on the train. It doesn't matter.

They / buy

B Pair work Two coworkers are at Penn Station, and they work in Oak Plains. It's 7:20 A.M. They have to arrive in Oak Plains for work at 9:00. Use the schedule to discuss all the possible choices. Use <u>could</u> and <u>should</u>. Explain your choices.

Blue numbers = express trains

Penn Station	Northway	Oak Plains	Carmel
7:15	7:50	8:30	9:00
7:25	—	8:25	8:55
7:30	—	—	8:55
7:30	8:05	8:45	9:15
7:50	8:25	9:05	9:35

❝ They could take the 7:30 express. ❞

❝ No. That train doesn't stop in Oak Plains. ❞

CONVERSATION MODEL

5:04

A 🔊 Read and listen to someone buying tickets.

A: Can I still make the 5:12 bus to Montreal?

B: I'm sorry. It left five minutes ago.

A: Too bad. What should I do?

B: Well, you could take the 5:30.

A: OK. One ticket, please.

B: One-way or round-trip?

A: Round-trip, please.

5:05

B 🔊 **Rhythm and intonation** Listen again and repeat. Then practice the Conversation Model with a partner.

NOW YOU CAN Discuss schedules and buy tickets

A Pair work Use the train departure board. Imagine it is now 7:15. Change the Conversation Model, based on where you want to go. Then change roles.

A: Can I still make the .... train to ....?

B: No, I'm sorry. It left .... minutes ago.

A: .... What should I do?

B: Well, you could take the ....

A: OK. One ticket, please.

B: One-way or round-trip?

A: ...., please.

Don't stop!
• Discuss the price of tickets.
• Ask whether the train makes stops.
• Ask for the kind of seat you'd like.

DEPARTURES 07:15 AM

TO	DEPARTS	TRACK
OSAKA	06:55	6
NARITA	07:03	9
KYOTO	07:12	19
OSAKA	08:23	8
NARITA	08:26	9
KYOTO	08:31	18

B Change partners Practice the conversation again. Discuss other departures.

GRAMMAR   *Be going to to express the future: Review*

base form

I'm going to   rent a car in New York.
She's going to   eat at the airport.
We're going to   take a taxi into town.

Are they going to need a taxi? (Yes, they are. / No, they aren't.)
Is Beth going to make a reservation? (Yes, she is. / No, she isn't.)

When are you going to arrive? (At noon.)   Who are they going to meet? (The travel agent.)
Where is he going to wait? (In the lobby.)   Who's going to take me to the airport? (Tom is.)

Remember: The present continuous is also often used to express future plans.
I'm renting a car in New York **next week**.

GRAMMAR BOOSTER ▸ p. 138
• *Expansion: future actions*

A Grammar practice Complete each statement or question with <u>be going to</u> and the base form of the verb.

1 .... tickets for the express. *they / buy*

2 When .... for the airport? *she / leave*

3 .... an aisle seat? *you / ask for*

4 Who .... him to the train station? *take*

B Complete the e-mail. Circle the correct verb forms.

> Here's my travel information: I (1 leaving / 'm leaving) Mexico City at 4:45 P.M.
> on Atlas Airlines flight 6702. The flight (2 is arriving / arriving) in Chicago at
> 9:50 P.M. Mara's flight (3 going to get in / is getting in) ten minutes later, so we
> (4 're meeting / meeting) at the baggage claim. That's too late for you to pick
> me up, so I (5 'm going to take / take) a limo from O'Hare. Mara
> (6 goes to / is going to) come along and (7 spend / spending) the night with
> us. Her flight to Tokyo (8 not leaving / isn't leaving) until the next day.

C Pair work Ask your partner three questions about his or her future plans. Use <u>be going to</u>.

❝ What are you going to do on your vacation? ❞

VOCABULARY   *Travel services*

A 🔊 *5:06* Read and listen. Then listen again and repeat.

a rental car

a taxi

a limousine / a limo

a hotel reservation

5:07 **◄))) Listening comprehension** Listen to the conversations. Then listen again and complete each sentence with <u>be going to</u> and infer the name of a travel service.

1 He .... (reserve) a
.... for her.

2 The tourist .... (need)
a .... in Seoul.

3 She .... (get) a
.... at John F. Kennedy Airport.

4 The agent .... (check) to
see if he can reserve a .... for the tourist.

CONVERSATION MODEL

A 5:08 **◄))** Read and listen to a conversation between a travel agent and a traveler.

A: Hello. Baker Travel. Can I help you?

B: I hope so. I'm going to need a car in Dubai.

A: Certainly. What date are you arriving?

B: April 6th.

A: And what time?

B: Let me check . . . 5:45 P.M.

B 5:09 **◄))) Rhythm and intonation** Listen again and repeat. Then practice the Conversation Model with a partner.

C Find the grammar Find and circle two ways that A and B express future plans in the Conversation Model.

NOW YOU CAN Book travel services

A Pair work Change the Conversation Model. Book one of the travel services from the Vocabulary. Use the tickets for arrival information. Then change roles.

A: Hello. Can I help you?

B: .... I'm going to need ....
in ....

A: .... What date are you arriving?

B: ....

A: And what time?

B: Let me check . . . .

> **Don't stop!**
> Ask for additional services.
>
> " I'm also going to need
> a hotel reservation. "

B Change partners Make your own flight, bus, or train tickets. Then practice the conversation again, using <u>your</u> tickets.

Your ticket

From _____

To _____

Date _____

Departs _____ Arrives _____

PASSENGER TICKET AND BAGGAGE CHECK
AIR CUZCO   APRIL 11   FLIGHT 22
DEPARTURE: 18:00   ARRIVAL: 19:15
LIMA TO CUZCO
88985376124   0 988 7631986534 7

Seoul Touristbus
FROM Seoul
TO Sokcho
DATE 13 August
DEPARTS 07:45
ARRIVES 11:55

BOARDING PASS
EXCELA RAIL TRANSPORT
JUNE 26 EXPRESS TRAIN
NEW YORK TO WASHINGTON
DEPARTURE: 6:00 PM
ARRIVAL: 9:10 PM

GOAL **Understand airport announcements**

BEFORE YOU LISTEN

A 🔊 5:10 **Vocabulary** • *Airline passenger information* Read and listen. Then listen again and repeat.

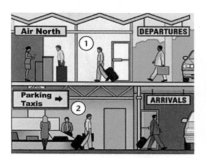

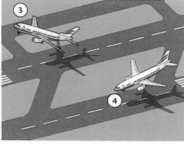

① **depart**   ② **arrive**   ③ **take off**   ④ **land**   ⑤ **go through security**

⑥ **the gate**   ⑦ **an agent**

⑧ **a boarding pass**   ⑨ **a passenger**

⑩ **the departure lounge**

Some flight problems
- The flight is **overbooked**. The airline sold too many tickets, so some passengers can't board.
- The flight is **delayed**. The flight will depart late.
- The flight is **canceled**. The passengers have to find another flight.

B Use the Vocabulary to complete the pre-flight instructions.

When you .... at the airport, you should take your luggage to the check-in counter and get
your .... Then you can ...., where .... have
to put all their hand luggage on the belt. From there you should go to the .... your plane is
departing from. If you are early and your plane hasn't landed or arrived at the gate, just have a seat in
the .... When your flight is called, you can show your boarding pass to the
.... and get on the plane. Be sure to turn off all electronic devices and put on your seat belt before
your plane .... from the gate. Enjoy the takeoff, and have a good flight!

LISTENING COMPREHENSION

A 🔊 5:11 **Understand public announcements** Listen to the
announcements. Check the travel problems.

☐ a delay   ☐ a gate change

☐ a cancellation   ☐ a security problem

☐ an overbooking   ☐ a mechanical problem

B 🔊)) **Listen for details** Listen again and write the flight information.

1 flight number: ....   **3** final departure gate: ....

2 original departure gate: ....   **4** final departure time: ....

PRONUNCIATION   *Intonation for stating alternatives*

A 🔊)) 5:13 Listen to the rhythm and intonation of alternatives. Then listen again and repeat.

1 Well, you could take the train or the bus.

2 They could wait or reserve a later flight.

3 Would you like one-way or round-trip?

B Now practice saying each sentence on your own.

NOW YOU CAN **Understand airport announcements**

A Read the announcement by the gate agent for
Rapid Air flight 58 from Brasilia to São Paulo.
Make sure you understand the details.

> 66 Good afternoon, ladies and gentlemen. Flight 58 is
> overbooked. We apologize. We need two volunteers to
> give up their seats on this flight. There are seats available
> on all later flights to São Paulo. If you volunteer to take a
> later flight, Rapid Air will give you a free round-trip ticket
> anywhere we fly. The free ticket is good for one year. 99

B **Pair work** Now act on the airport announcement.
Imagine that you and your partner have tickets on
flight 58. First read the situation:

- The time is now 16:35.
- You have a very important dinner in São Paulo at 20:30.
- The flight takes about two hours gate to gate.

Then look at the departure schedule
and discuss your alternatives.

DEPARTURES			
São Paulo	56	16:20	departed
Rio de Janeiro	89	16:40	boarding
São Paulo	58	16:50	now 17:25
São Paulo	60	17:50	on time

C **Discussion** Summarize your decision for
the class and explain why you made that
decision. How many students decided to
take a later flight?

We could volunteer. Flight 60
is going to arrive before the
dinner. What do you think?

I don't know. I think we should stay on
flight 58. There's always a lot of traffic
and we'll be late for the dinner.

BEFORE YOU READ

A 🔊 5:14 **Vocabulary** • *Transportation problems* Read and listen. Then listen again and repeat.

We **had an accident**.

We **had mechanical problems**.

We **missed** our **train**.

We **got bumped from** the **flight**.

We **got seasick**.

Also:
carsick
airsick

B 🔊 5:15 **Listening comprehension** Listen and complete each statement with the Vocabulary.

1 They ....

2 They ....

3 They ....

4 They ....

5 They ....

READING 🔊 5:16

GOT BUMPED FROM A FLIGHT?
Maybe it's not so bad after all...

As most travelers know, airlines commonly overbook flights because of the large and predictable number of "no-shows"—people who have reservations but don't show up for the flight. Overbooking helps airlines limit the number of empty seats on their flights. However, if a flight is overbooked, some passengers with confirmed reservations have to get off the plane.

Getting bumped isn't always a bad thing, however. There is a growing number of passengers who feel lucky if their flight is overbooked. Why? Because airlines have to provide bumped passengers with cash, free flights, hotels, and/or meals to compensate them for their inconvenience.

In fact, airlines usually ask for volunteers to get off an overbooked flight in exchange for those perks, and many passengers say "Sure!" and happily deplane. Some people even make a habit of choosing flights that are likely to be overbooked, just so they can volunteer!

Source: Adapted from airconsumer.ost.gov

Driver blames GPS for train crash

BEDFORD HILLS–Last night, Edward Carter, 43, of White Plains told police that his car's global positioning system (GPS) instructed him to make a wrong turn directly onto the train tracks in Bedford Hills. When he turned, his car became stuck on the track, and he had to abandon the car.

In a statement to the police, the man said he was driving north with his son on the Saw Mill Parkway at about 8 P.M. They planned to go to a restaurant

The location of last night's accident

on Route 117. Following the instructions from his GPS unit, he exited the parkway at Green Lane. But then, instead of driving to Route 117 and turning right there, he made a very wrong turn. He turned right at the railroad tracks. The man and his son tried to move the car off the tracks, but they couldn't. Shortly afterward, a Metro-North commuter train hit Mr. Carter's car. Luckily, there were no deaths or injuries. Police say that drivers need to pay attention to the road, not the GPS unit.

Source: Adapted from news articles in lohud.com

Critical thinking Based on the Reading and your own ideas, discuss the following topics.

1 Why do you think people with confirmed reservations become "no-shows"?

2 What are some advantages of getting bumped? Would you volunteer to get off an overbooked flight? Explain.

3 What are some advantages of GPS systems? What are some disadvantages?

4 Do you prefer GPS systems or paper maps? Explain.

On your *ActiveBook* Self-Study Disc:
Extra Reading Comprehension Questions

NOW YOU CAN   Describe transportation problems

A Check all the means of transportation you have taken. Then add other means you know.

☐ bus   ☐ train   ☐ taxi   ☐ limousine   ☐ ferry

☐ ship   ☐ airplane   ☐ helicopter   ☐ other ....

B **Pair work** Ask your partner questions about the means of transportation he or she checked.

> " When was the last time you took a train? "

C **Notepadding** Choose a time when you had transportation problems. On the notepad, make notes about the trip.

means of transportation:	
month, day, or year of trip:	
destination:	
bad memories:	

D **Group work** Now tell your story to your classmates. Describe your transportation problems. Ask them questions about their problems.

> You won't believe what happened on my trip. First, I got carsick in the airport limo. Then…

 Be sure to recycle this language.

Problems

The ___ was terrible.
The ___ were unfriendly.
They canceled my ___ .
The ___ didn't work.
They lost my ___ .

Someone stole my ___ .
The ___ drove me crazy.
The [flight] was bumpy / scary.
The [drive] was long / boring.

Responses
What was wrong with the ___ ?
I'm sorry to hear that.
That's a shame / too bad.

Review

A 5:17 🔊 **Listening comprehension** It's 7:26 A.M. now. Listen as you look at the departure board. Then listen again and use reasoning to determine if each statement is true or false. Circle T (<u>true</u>) or F (<u>false</u>).

T F **1** They could take the 8:31.

T F **2** They should take the 8:25.

T F **3** They're going to Boston.

T F **4** They're both going to take the train to Washington.

T F **5** He usually takes the 7:25.

T F **6** They should hurry.

DEPARTURES		7:26 A.M.
TO	DEPARTS	TRACK
WASHINGTON	7:10	6
BOSTON	7:22	9
PHILADELPHIA	7:25	19
WASHINGTON	8:25	8
BOSTON	8:26	24
PHILADELPHIA	8:31	18

B Complete each statement with a correct word or phrase.

1 It's important to make a .... early because it can be difficult to find a room after you arrive.

2 When your whole family is going to the airport together, you can reserve a .... It's usually very comfortable and has space for all of your luggage.

3 It can be convenient to use a .... if you want to drive but can't bring your own car.

4 Do you think I should take the .... train? I know it's much faster, but I'm not sure it stops at my station on weekends.

5 My husband always gets .... seat. He likes to get up and walk around on long flights.

6 I hope it's a .... flight. I get really scared every time the plane takes off or lands.

7 It's not a non-stop, but it's a .... flight. You don't have to change planes, but the plane stops twice.

8 Are you kidding? They .... it? That was the last flight! Just ten minutes ago they said it was here and ready to board!

9 The airline .... the flight, and when I got to the gate, the agent said another passenger had my seat. I had such bad luck!

5:18/5:19
🎵 **Top Notch Pop**
"Five Hundred Ways"
Lyrics p. 150

C Complete the conversation with <u>be going to</u> and the indicated verbs.

A: On Saturday, ... for Cancún.
       1 we / leave

B: Really? .... a car there? There are some
       2 you / rent
    great places to explore.

A: No. I think .... on the beach and rest.
       3 we / stay
    By the way, where .... for your vacation?
       4 you and Margo / go

B: I'm not sure. But .... to Bangkok on
       5 I / travel
    business next month, and .... a few days
       6 I / take
    off to go sightseeing. I hear it's great.

D **Writing** On a separate sheet of paper, write two paragraphs—one about your most recent trip and one about your next trip. In the first paragraph, describe the transportation you took and write about any problems you had. In the second paragraph, write about the transportation you plan to take. Use <u>be going to</u>.

WRITING BOOSTER ▸ p. 147

• *The paragraph*
• *Guidance for Exercise D*

Contest Form teams. Create questions about the trip to ask another team. (One point for each correct question and one point for each correct answer.)

Role play Choose one picture. Create a conversation for the people. Use <u>could</u> and <u>should</u>. For example:

Agent: You could go to Hawaii or ...

Group story Take turns telling the story in the pictures. Each student adds one sentence.

NOW I CAN...

☐ Discuss schedules and buy tickets.
☐ Book travel services.
☐ Understand airport announcements.
☐ Describe transportation problems.

109

Shopping Smart

GOALS After Unit 10, you will be a

1 Ask for a recommendation.
2 Bargain for a lower price.
3 Discuss showing appreciation for se
4 Describe where to get the best dea

Get the Best Exchange Rate

Before you travel to another country, check the exchange rate of your currency against the currency of the foreign country you're visiting. During your trip, you'll get the best rate if you buy foreign currency with an ATM card or a credit card.

However, if you have to exchange cash, the best rates are usually at banks and post offices.

When possible, use a credit card for larger expenses such as hotel bills, tickets, and car rentals. But be careful—many credit card companies now add fees for these transactions. Use an ATM card for your daily cash needs. But check with your bank before you leave to make sure you can use your card in the country you are visiting. Also ask if they charge extra for using your card there.

VISTAcard		Monthly Statement
Date	Transaction	Debit
10/07	CAFÉ LUNA	200.00
10/06	*FOREIGN TRANSACTION FEE	4.68
10/06	HOTEL DE CALLAO	180.00

Source: independenttraveler.com

A 🔊 5:20 **Vocabulary • Financial terms**
Listen and repeat.

- an ATM
- cash
- foreign currency
- a currency exchange
- an exchange rate
- a fee

B Pair work Discuss your spending habits. Ask and answer the following questions.

1 Do you make purchases with a credit card? When?

2 What do you usually buy with cash?

3 Do you ever exchange money for foreign currency? When? How?

ENGLISH FOR TODAY'S WORLD
connecting people from different cultures
and language backgrounds

C ◀)) **Photo story** Read and listen to people shopping for souvenirs.

5:21

Jenn: Oh, no. I'm almost out of cash. And I want to get a gift for my mom. I sure hope these shops accept credit cards.

Pat: I'll bet they do. Let's go in here. They have some really nice stuff.

Jenn: Great!

Pat: Hey, what do you think of this?

Jenn: It's gorgeous. But it's a bit more than I want to spend.

Pat: Maybe you can get a better price. It can't hurt to ask.

Jenn: I don't know. I'm not very good at bargaining.

Clerk: Excuse me. Maybe I can help. Let me show you something more affordable.

Jenn: Oh, that one's nice, too. How much do you want for it?

Clerk: Well, the lowest I could go is forty euros.

Jenn: I'll take it. You do accept credit cards, don't you?

Clerk: Sorry, no. But there is an ATM right across the street.

Clerk: Italian speaker

D Focus on language Find an underlined statement in the Photo Story with the same meaning as each of the following:

1 I'd prefer something cheaper. ....

2 This shop sells good things. ....

3 I'll sell it to you for . . . .

4 I don't know how to ask for a lower price. ....

5 I don't have much money. ....

6 Don't be afraid to bargain. ....

7 Here's a cheaper one. ....

E Discussion Are you good at bargaining? How do you get a good price when you go shopping?

F Pair work Complete the chart with your own opinions of the advantages and disadvantages of credit cards and cash. Then discuss your ideas with a partner.

An advantage of credit cards:	
A disadvantage of credit cards:	
An advantage of cash:	
A disadvantage of cash:	

GOAL | Ask for a recommendation

GRAMMAR / *Superlative adjectives*

Irregular forms		
good →	better (than) →	the best
bad →	worse (than) →	the worst

Use superlative adjectives to compare more than two people, places, things, or ideas.

Which projector is the cheapest of these three?
Which brands are the most popular in your store?

adjective	comparative	superlative	adjective	comparative	superlative
cheap	cheaper (than)	the cheapest	comfortable	more comfortable (than)	the most comfortable
nice	nicer (than)	the nicest	portable	more portable (than)	the most portable
easy	easier (than)	the easiest	difficult	less difficult (than)	the least difficult
big	bigger (than)	the biggest	expensive	less expensive (than)	the least expensive

GRAMMAR BOOSTER ▸ p. 139

Comparatives and superlatives: usage and form

A Grammar practice Read the salesperson's recommendations. Complete each statement, using the superlative form of the adjective.

1 The Aptex is .... of our MP3 players.
   new

2 The Focus C20 is very inexpensive. It's .... digital camera we sell.
   cheap

3 Compared to our other camcorders, the Manko 210 is ....
   easy to use

4 The Focus C50 is .... digital camera we sell.
   popular

5 The Vista PX is .... camcorder you can buy.
   light

6 Our customers say the iSong is .... MP3 player available today.
   practical

7 You'll like the Manko 230 MP3 player. It's .... to use.
   difficult

8 If you don't want to spend a lot, the Raxx is .... camcorder you can buy.
   expensive

9 If you want the best but don't care about cost, the Vista LS is ....
   expensive
   camcorder we have.

B Complete the conversations. Use the superlative form of the adjectives.

1 A: All of these cameras are easy to use.
   B: But which is ....?
      small

2 A: All of our ski sweaters are pretty warm.
   B: But I want a really heavy one. Which brand makes .... ones?
      heavy

3 A: She wrote at least six books about Italy.
   B: I know. But which of her books is ....?
      interesting

4 A: Do you want to take a taxi, bus, or train to the airport?
   B: Which is ....?
      convenient

5 A: You can study English at any school you want.
   B: All three sound great. But which school is ....?
      popular

6 A: Here are three vacation packages you can choose from.
   B: That's nice. But just tell me which one is ....
      affordable

A 🔊 5:22 Read and listen to someone asking for a recommendation.

A: I'm looking for a digital camera. Which is the least expensive?

B: The B100. But it's not the best. How much can you spend?

A: No more than 250.

B: Well, we have some good ones in your price range.

A: Great! Can I have a look?

B 🔊 5:23 **Rhythm and intonation** Listen again and repeat. Then practice the Conversation Model with a partner.

NOW YOU CAN   Ask for a recommendation

A Pair work Change the Conversation Model. Use the ads, or other real ads, to ask for a recommendation. Use superlative adjectives. Then change roles.

Ideas
• nice
• popular
• light
• practical
• easy to use

A: I'm looking for .... Which is the .... ?

B: The .... But it's not the .... How much can you spend?

A: No more than ....

B: Well, ...

A: ....

> **Don't stop!** **Continue the conversation.**
> I'm also looking for [an MP3 player].
> Tell me about [the Prego 5].
> Do you accept credit cards?
> Is there an ATM nearby?
> I think I'll take the [X23].
> Could you gift wrap it for me?

B Change partners Ask about other electronic products.

C Extension Bring in newspaper ads for electronic and other products. Use both comparative and superlative adjectives to discuss them.

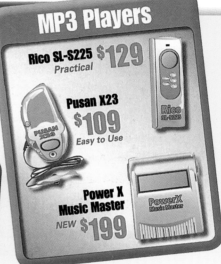

MP3 Players

Rico SL-S225 $129
Practical

Pusan X23 $109
Easy to Use

Power X Music Master
NEW $199

Camcorders

Vision 720 $949
Very Light

Pusan 5X $829
Easy to Use

Diego P500 $299
Popular

Digital Cameras

Honshu X24 $209
Very Popular

Honshu B100 $149

Prego 5 $299
NEW

| GOAL | Bargain for a lower price |

CONVERSATION MODEL

A 🔊 5:24 Read and listen to someone bargaining for a lower price.

A: How much do you want for that rug?

B: This one?

A: No. That one's not big enough.
The other one.

B: 300.

A: That's a lot more than I want to spend.
I can give you 200.

B: How about 225?

A: OK. That sounds fair.

B 🔊 5:25 **Rhythm and intonation** Listen again and repeat. Then practice the Conversation Model with a partner.

GRAMMAR   _Too_ and _enough_

When something is not satisfactory:
Those rugs are too small.   OR   Those rugs aren't big enough.
That camera is too heavy.   OR   That camera isn't light enough.

When something is satisfactory:
This MP3 player is small enough. I'll take it.

Be careful!
Don't say: This MP3 player is

> **GRAMMAR BOOSTER** ▸ p. 140
> • Usage: _too_, _really_, and _very_

Grammar practice Read the conversations between customers and salespeople. Then complete each conversation. Use _too_ or _enough_ and an adjective from the list.

Adjectives
slow
fast
cheap
expensive
quiet
noisy
small
big
light
heavy

1 A: Are you sure this microwave is ....? I'm a pretty busy guy.
   B: Absolutely. The X11 is our fastest model.

2 A: These shoes aren't .... They're very uncomfortable.
   B: I'm so sorry. Let me get you a bigger size.

3 A: My photocopier is .... It's driving me crazy!
   B: Then let me show you a model that's quieter.

4 A: I bought these portable speakers last week, but they really aren't
   .... for travel.
   B: Don't worry. You can exchange them for another pair that's not so heavy.

5 A: How about this MP3 player? It's pretty small.
   B: That's definitely .... I'll take it.

6 A: This jacket is a real bargain, sir. It's only $692.
   B: $692? That's .... I don't want to spend that much.

A 🔊 5:26 Listen to how rising intonation is used to ask for clarification. Then listen again and repeat.

1 A: Could I have a look at those bowls?

   B: These small ones? ↗

   A: No, the big ones.

2 A: How much is that vase?

   B: This green one? ↗

   A: That's right.

B **Pair work** Place some objects on your desk. Ask to have a look, and practice using rising intonation to ask for clarification.

   ❝ Could I have a look at those sunglasses? ❞

   ❝ These brown ones? ❞

A 🔊 5:27 Read and listen. Then listen again and repeat.

Buyer's language	Seller's language
• **How much do you want for that** [shawl]?	• **How much do you want to spend?**
• **That's more than I want to spend.**	• **I could go as low as** [seventy].
• **I can give you** [twenty] **for it.**	• **I can't go lower than** [sixty].
• **Would you take** [thirty]?	• **You can have it for** [fifty].
• **All I have is** [forty].	• **How about** [forty-five]?
• **It's a deal.**	• **It's a deal.**

B 🔊 5:28 **Listening comprehension** Listen to people bargaining. Complete each statement with the amount they agreed on and the item bought.

1 The buyer pays …….. for the …………… .

2 The buyer pays …….. for the …………… .

3 The buyer pays …….. for the …………… .

4 The buyer pays …….. for the …………… .

NOW YOU CAN   Bargain for a lower price

A **Role play** Imagine that you are in a place where bargaining is common. One of you is the buyer, and the other is the seller. Use the Vocabulary and the photos, or your own ideas. Then change roles. Start like this:

   A: How much do you want for …….. ?

   Don't stop!
   • Ask about size, color, etc.
   • Use <u>too</u> and <u>enough</u>.
   • Use superlatives.

B **Change partners** Bargain for one of the other items.

Warm-up In your opinion, why is it important to understand the customs of other countries?

READING 5:29

When Should I Tip?

It's the question every traveler asks.

In some countries around the world, tipping isn't customary. But there are at least 180 countries where travelers need to know the rules. In some places, like China, where tipping was not the custom in the past, that's changing. In most other countries, tipping is customary—but the rules can be quite complicated.

Restaurants

In the U.S., restaurant servers expect a tip of 15 to 20% of the check—depending on how satisfied you are with the service. In most other countries, however, it's about 10%. In the U.S., you leave your tip on the table. But in Austria and Germany, it's considered rude if you don't hand the tip directly to the server.

In Europe, restaurants almost always add a service charge to the check, so you don't need to leave a separate tip. But in the U.S., a service charge is only added for groups of six or more people. So it's a good idea to look carefully at your check!

And if that's not complicated enough, think about this: In some countries, like Italy and Venezuela, restaurants add a service charge to the bill, but an additional 5 to 10% tip is still expected!

Taxis

In the U.S. and Canada, you always tip taxi drivers 15% of the taxi fare. However, in South America and many European countries, you don't usually tip them. Instead, you can round off the fare and say, "Keep the change."

Hotels

What about the porter who carries your luggage? In Australia, you tip about AUS $3 (US $2) per bag. But in most countries, a tip of about US $1 will be fine. You can also leave about US $1 to $2 a day for the maid who cleans your hotel room.

So what should travelers do? Check the Internet for information on tipping customs before you leave. As the famous saying goes, "When in Rome, do as the Romans do." But remember: You never have to tip if the service is terrible.

FOR YOUR INFORMATION

Never tip in these countries:

Japan	Singapore
Korea	Thailand
Malaysia	United Arab Emirates
New Zealand	Vietnam

Information source: cnn.com

A Draw conclusions Read each person's question. Give advice, according to the Reading. Then find the place in the Reading where the information comes from.

> 66 I'm going to Warsaw, Poland. I'm staying in a nice hotel for about six days. How much should I tip the maid? 99

> 66 I'm going to Chicago, in the U.S., on business. Let's say I take ten clients out for lunch and the bill is US $400. How much more should I leave for the tip? 99

> 66 I'm flying to Melbourne, Australia, next week. I have three large bags. If a porter helps me, how much should I tip? 99

> 66 I'm going to be in Toronto, Canada, this weekend. Someone told me the fare from the airport is CAN $43. How much should I tip the driver? 99

B Apply information Imagine that you are visiting one of the countries in the Reading. Describe a situation in a restaurant, a hotel, or a taxi. Your classmates decide how much to tip.

On your *ActiveBook* Self-Study Disc:
Extra Reading Comprehension Questions

NOW YOU CAN Discuss showing appreciation for service

A Frame your ideas Check the ways you have shown appreciation to someone for good service. Then tell a partner about some of them.

☐ I left a tip.
☐ I gave a gift.
☐ I said "Thank you."
☐ I wrote a "thank-you" note.
☐ I wrote a letter to the manager.
☐ Other: _____

> 66 Last year, I went to a restaurant where the waiter was really nice. At the end of the meal, I spoke to the manager about his great service. 99

B Notepadding With a partner, write suggestions to a visitor to your country for how to show appreciation for good service. If tipping is customary, explain how much to tip.

Restaurant servers:	
Taxi drivers:	
Hotel maids:	
Baggage porters:	
Hairdressers:	
Office assistants:	
Other:	

C Discussion Now discuss how to show appreciation for good service in your country. What are the customs? Does everyone agree?

Text-mining (optional)
Underline language in the Reading on page 116 to use in the Discussion. For example:

"[Restaurant servers] expect a tip of ..."

| GOAL | Describe where to get the best deals |

BEFORE YOU LISTEN

A 🔊 5:30 **Vocabulary** • *How to describe good and bad deals* Read and listen. Then listen again and repeat.

Good deals

She **got a great deal.**
She **saved a lot of money.**
It **was a real bargain.**

Bad deals

He **got a bad deal.**
He **paid too much money.**
It **was a total rip-off.**

B **Discussion** Read about two shopping experiences. Do you think either of the people got a good deal? Use the Vocabulary.

I was in Saudi Arabia on business, and I wanted to buy a rug. I found a beautiful one, but the asking price was too high: US $900. I said I could go as high as $350. We bargained for a long time, but the merchant wouldn't come down in price. Finally, we shook hands. When I turned to leave the store, he was very surprised. I thought the handshake meant "Sorry. That's too low." But it really meant "It's a deal." So I went back in and bought it.

When I was in Shanghai, I decided to look for some antique pottery. I found a beautiful blue and white vase from the sixteenth-century Ming Dynasty. We bargained about the price, and the salesperson came way down for me. So of course I bought it. It was more than I wanted to spend, but I really liked it. Later, a friend told me that the "antiques" in these shops aren't really antiques—they're actually new!

LISTENING COMPREHENSION

A 🔊 5:31 **Listen for main ideas** Listen to the conversations about shopping. Then listen again and complete the chart.

	What did the shopper buy?	Did the shopper get a good price?	
1		☐ yes	☐ no
2		☐ yes	☐ no
3		☐ yes	☐ no
4		☐ yes	☐ no

B 🔊 **Listen for details** Listen again. Write the price each person paid.

1 ……… euros   **2** ……… pounds   **3** ……… dollars   **4** ……… pesos

NOW YOU CAN | Describe where to get the best deals

A Notepadding Write notes about a good or bad shopping experience you have had.

What did you buy?
Where did you buy it?
Did you bargain?
How much did you pay?

B Group work Now describe your shopping experience to your classmates. Use your notepad.

Text-mining (optional)
Underline language in the stories in Exercise B on page 118 to use in the Group Work. For example:
"We bargained for a long time …"

C Frame your ideas Complete the chart with places in your city or town.

What are . . .	Where can you buy . . .
the best restaurants?	the least expensive fruits and vegetables?
the nicest hotels?	the most beautiful flowers?
the most expensive department stores?	the best electronic products?
the most unusual markets?	the most unusual souvenirs?
the most interesting museums?	the wildest clothes?

D Discussion Where should people go in your city or town for the best deals?

> ❝ The fruits and vegetables at the North Market are the freshest in town. ❞

Review

A 🔊 **Listening comprehension** Listen to each conversation. Write the item that the people are talking about. Indicate whether the item is satisfactory (✓) or unsatisfactory (✗) to the customer. Then listen again and circle the adjectives that the salesperson uses to describe the product.

	They're talking about . . .	Satisfactory?	Adjectives
1		☐	light / fast / cheap
2		☐	light / warm / beautiful
3		☐	tall / beautiful / affordable
4		☐	light / easy to use / affordable

B Complete the sentences.

1 If you're out of cash and the bank is closed, you can get money from ....

2 If there's a service charge on the bill, you probably don't need to leave ....

3 In some places, you can .... for a lower price.

4 Before you go overseas, you should check the .... of your currency and the currency of the place you're traveling.

5 It was a real .... I saved a lot of money.

6 It was a total .... I paid too much money.

C On a separate sheet of paper, rewrite each sentence, using <u>too</u> or <u>enough</u>. For example:

That vase is too heavy.

That vase isn't light enough.

1 Those cameras aren't cheap enough.

2 This printer is too slow.

3 The inside of the fridge isn't cool enough.

4 That restaurant is too noisy.

5 My flat screen TV isn't big enough.

6 Those pants aren't long enough.

D Write two sentences about shopping in your city. Use the superlative.

The stores in Old Town have the most interesting gifts.

1	
2	

5:34/5:35
Top Notch Pop
"Shopping for Souvenirs"
Lyrics p. 150

E **Writing** On a separate sheet of paper, write a guide to the best places for a visitor to your city or town to stay in, visit, and shop.

Ideas
hotels   theaters
stores   neighborhoods
museums   stadiums

WRITING BOOSTER ▸ p. 148

• *Connecting contradictory ideas*
• *Guidance for Exercise E*

Al's Electronics

CoolRay 6
Super thin
US $350

Now US $220
Easy to use
Only 3 oz / .085 kg

Basik XT
So Fast!
US $980

Now US $950
Very Professional
Only 24 oz / .68 kg

EasyPix 500
Very Popular
US $220

Now US $180
Only 4.1 oz / .12 kg

Dazio 420
Brightness: 2000 lumens
Very portable
US $1,199

Now US $999
Only 2.8 lb / 1.27 kg

Clearview 3Z
Brightness: 2000 lumens
Really affordable
US $899

Now US $849
Only 4 lb / 1.81 kg

Manna T-20
Brightness: 4000 lumens
So powerful!
US $3,999

Now US $3,899
Only 3.5 lb / 1.59 kg

Cloud 9
50" / 127 cm
Like it loud? This is the one!
US $1,399

Now US $1,149

Runex
19" / 48 cm
Very portable
US $399

Now US $229

Washburn
32" / 81 cm
Brand new!
US $699

Now US $599

ORAL REVIEW

Contest Form teams. Create false statements about the products. Another team corrects the statements. (Teams get one point for each statement they correct.) For example:

> There's a sale on camcorders today.

Role play Create conversations for the people.
- Ask for a recommendation. Start like this:
  > I'm looking for ___. Which is the . . . ?
- Bargain for the best price. Start like this:
  > How much do you want for that . . . ?

GIFTS 'N THINGS

NOW I CAN...

- ☐ Ask for a recommendation.
- ☐ Bargain for a lower price.
- ☐ Discuss showing appreciation for service.
- ☐ Describe where to get the best deals.

121

Reference Charts

Countries and nationalities

Argentina	Argentinean / Argentine	Guatemala	Guatemalan	Peru	Peruvian
Australia	Australian	Holland	Dutch	Poland	Polish
Belgium	Belgian	Honduras	Honduran	Portugal	Portuguese
Bolivia	Bolivian	Hungary	Hungarian	Russia	Russian
Brazil	Brazilian	India	Indian	Saudi Arabia	Saudi / Saudi Arabian
Canada	Canadian	Indonesia	Indonesian	Spain	Spanish
Chile	Chilean	Ireland	Irish	Sweden	Swedish
China	Chinese	Italy	Italian	Switzerland	Swiss
Colombia	Colombian	Japan	Japanese	Taiwan	Chinese
Costa Rica	Costa Rican	Korea	Korean	Thailand	Thai
Ecuador	Ecuadorian	Lebanon	Lebanese	Turkey	Turkish
Egypt	Egyptian	Malaysia	Malaysian	the United Kingdom	British
El Salvador	Salvadorean	Mexico	Mexican	the United States	American
France	French	Nicaragua	Nicaraguan	Uruguay	Uruguayan
Germany	German	Panama	Panamanian	Venezuela	Venezuelan
Greece	Greek	Paraguay	Paraguayan	Vietnam	Vietnamese

Non-count nouns

This list is an at-a-glance reference to the non-count nouns used in *Top Notch 1*.

aerobics	cheese	entertainment	ice	oil	service	traffic
air-conditioning	chicken	fish	ice cream	outerwear	shopping	transportation
basketball	clothing	food	juice	pasta	shrimp	TV
beef	coffee	fruit	junk food	pepper	sightseeing	walking
bike riding	crab	garlic	lamb	pie	skydiving	water
bread	culture	golf	lettuce	rice	sleepwear	weather
broccoli	danger	health	lingerie	running	soccer	wildlife
butter	dessert	history	meat	salad	soup	yogurt
cake	dinner	hosiery	milk	salt	squid	
candy	electronics	hot sauce	music	sausage	swimming	
cash	English	housework	nature	seafood	tennis	

Irregular verbs

base form	simple past	past participle	base form	simple past	past participle	base form	simple past	past participle
be	was / were	been	give	gave	given	sell	sold	sold
begin	began	begun	go	went	gone	send	sent	sent
break	broke	broken	grow	grew	grown	shake	shook	shaken
bring	brought	brought	have	had	had	sing	sang	sung
build	built	built	hear	heard	heard	sit	sat	sat
buy	bought	bought	hit	hit	hit	sleep	slept	slept
catch	caught	caught	hurt	hurt	hurt	speak	spoke	spoken
choose	chose	chosen	keep	kept	kept	spend	spent	spent
come	came	come	know	knew	known	stand	stood	stood
cost	cost	cost	leave	left	left	steal	stole	stolen
cut	cut	cut	lose	lost	lost	swim	swam	swum
do	did	done	make	made	made	take	took	taken
drink	drank	drunk	mean	meant	meant	teach	taught	taught
drive	drove	driven	meet	met	met	tell	told	told
eat	ate	eaten	pay	paid	paid	think	thought	thought
fall	fell	fallen	put	put	put	throw	threw	thrown
feel	felt	felt	quit	quit	quit	understand	understood	understood
find	found	found	read	read	read	wake up	woke up	woken up
fit	fit	fit	ride	rode	ridden	wear	wore	worn
fly	flew	flown	run	ran	run	win	won	won
forget	forgot	forgotten	say	said	said	write	wrote	written
get	got	gotten	see	saw	seen			

TOP NOTCH
1B
Grammar Booster

Grammar Booster

The Grammar Booster is optional. It is not required for the achievement tests in the *Top Notch Complete Assessment Package.* If you use the Grammar Booster, there are extra exercises in the Workbook in a separate labeled Grammar Booster section.

UNIT 6   Lesson 1

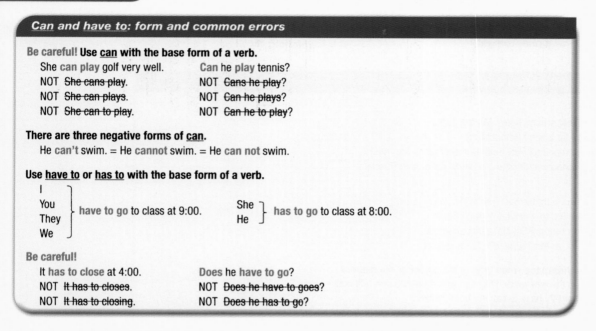

Can and have to: form and common errors

Be careful! Use can with the base form of a verb.

She **can play** golf very well.
NOT ~~She cans play.~~
NOT ~~She can plays.~~
NOT ~~She can to play.~~

Can he **play** tennis?
NOT ~~Cans he play?~~
NOT ~~Can he plays?~~
NOT ~~Can he to play?~~

There are three negative forms of can.

He **can't** swim. = He **cannot** swim. = He **can not** swim.

Use have to or has to with the base form of a verb.

I
You
They
We
} **have to go** to class at 9:00.

She
He
} **has to go** to class at 8:00.

Be careful!

It **has to close** at 4:00.
NOT ~~It has to closes.~~
NOT ~~It has to closing.~~

Does he **have to go**?
NOT ~~Does he have to goes?~~
NOT ~~Does he has to go?~~

A **Correct the following sentences.**

1 Can they ~~coming~~ *come* to the movie next week?

2 My mother-in-law have to go shopping this afternoon.

3 My cousin can't plays soccer tomorrow.

4 Does he has to meet his niece at the airport?

5 We're going to the beach this weekend, but I no can swim.

6 Alex can to go out for dinner tonight.

7 She doesn't have to working late tomorrow.

She cans go out for dinner.

8 Can he visits his in-laws next weekend?

9 You have to filling out an application for your English class.

10 Do we have to studying now? We're watching TV.

Can and have to: information questions

Can

Where **can** I **play** soccer around here? (Try the park.)
When **can** they **come** for lunch? (After class.)
How often **can** we **go** running? (Any time. Our afternoons are free.)
What languages **can** she **speak**? (She can speak Italian and Russian.)

Have to

What **does** he **have to do** tomorrow? (He has to go shopping.)
How often **does** she **have to work** late? (Not often.)
When **do** they **have to buy** the tickets? (This afternoon.)
Where **do** you **have to go** this morning? (To the airport.)

Be careful! **See the difference when Who is the object or the subject.**
Who **can** they **visit** on the weekend? They can visit their cousins. (object)
Who **do** you **have to call**? I have to call my boss. (object)
Who **can visit** his cousin on the weekend? John can. (subject)
Who **has to write** the report? My boss does. (subject)

B **Complete the questions, using the cues and can.**

1 A: _____ basketball around here? (Where / I / play)
  B: Try the school. It isn't far.

2 A: _____ dinner together? (When / we / have)
  B: How about tomorrow night?

3 A: I need some fresh air. _____ walking? (Where / I / go)
  B: You can go to the park. It's very nice.

4 A: _____ English? (How often / you / study)
  B: Not as much as I'd like to. I'm too busy.

5 A: _____ breakfast tomorrow morning? (Who / make)
  B: What about Bill? He always wakes up early.

6 A: _____ with about English classes? (Who / I / speak)
  B: The receptionist can help you.

C **Complete the questions and answers, using have to or has to.**

1 A: _____ he _____ (do) tomorrow?
  B: He _____ (go) to class.

2 A: _____ she _____ (call) the office?
  B: She _____ (call) every morning.

3 A: _____ he _____ (go) to the airport?
  B: He _____ (leave) here at 3:00.

4 A: _____ they _____ (send) the form to?
  B: They can't send it. They _____ (take) it to the office.

5 A: _____ you _____ (meet) after class?
  B: I _____ (meet) my sister. We're going to the movies.

6 A: _____ (help) the teacher after class?
  B: Chris and Tania. They _____ (clean) the board.

Can and be able to: present and past forms

You can also use **be able to** + base form for ability or possibility. **Can** is more frequent in spoken language.

I **can play** the violin. = I'm **able to play** the violin. (ability)
Bill **can meet** you at six. = Bill **is able to meet** you at six. (possibility)
They **can't call** this afternoon. = They **aren't able to call** this afternoon. (possibility)
He **can't fix** cars. = He **isn't able to fix** cars. (ability)

Use **could** or **was / were able to** + base form to talk about the past.

When I was four I **could swim** (or **was able to swim**).
They **could speak** (or **were able to speak**) French before they were ten.
She **couldn't be** (or **wasn't able to be**) there yesterday because she had a meeting.
We **couldn't understand** (or **weren't able to understand**) the directions.

Be careful! Use **was / were able to** (NOT **could**) for affirmative past statements of **possibility**.

She **was able to be** there yesterday. NOT She ~~could be~~ there yesterday.

D **On a separate sheet of paper, change can to be able to in the following sentences.**

1 She can swim very well.

2 They can't ride a bicycle.

3 George can meet you at the airport.

4 Lucy can't take the bus to the mall.

E **On a separate sheet of paper, change the following statements from the present to the past.**

1 We're able to help him.

2 The Martins can't go to the concert.

3 She is able to be there at seven.

4 Nicole can cook for the party.

5 Rachel and Brooke aren't able to play basketball at the school.

UNIT 6   Lesson 2

The simple present tense: non-action verbs

Some verbs are non-action verbs. Most non-action verbs are not usually used in the present continuous, even when they are describing something that is happening right now.

I **want** a sandwich. NOT I ~~am wanting~~ a sandwich.

Some non-action verbs have action and non-action meanings.

non-action meaning	action meaning
I **have** two sandwiches. (possession)	I'm **having** a sandwich. (eating)
I **think** English is easy. (opinion)	I'm **thinking** about her. (the act of thinking)

Some non-action verbs	
be	miss
have	need
know	see
like	understand
love	want

A **Complete the letter. Use the simple present tense or the present continuous form of the verbs.**

Dear Keith,
   It's 2:00 and I _____ (1 think) of you. The kids _____
(2 play) outside. I _____ (3 see) them through the window right
now. They _____ (4 have) a small table and chairs and they
_____ (5 have) a late lunch. I _____ (6 want) to send this
before I go to work. I _____ (7 know) you're working hard and we all
_____ (8 miss) you.
Maggie

The simple present tense: placement of frequency adverbs

Frequency adverbs generally go after the verb <u>be</u> and before other verbs.
I am usually at the pool on Saturdays.
I usually go to the pool on Saturdays.

<u>Sometimes</u>, <u>usually</u>, <u>often</u>, <u>generally</u>, and <u>occasionally</u> can also go at the beginning or end of a sentence.
Sometimes I go to the mall on Saturdays.
I go to the pool occasionally.

Be careful! Don't use <u>never</u> or <u>always</u> at the beginning or end of a sentence.
Don't say: ~~Never I go to the pool.~~ OR ~~I go to the pool always~~.

In negative sentences, most frequency adverbs can go before or after <u>don't</u> or <u>doesn't</u>.
Hank usually doesn't go running on the weekend.
Hank doesn't usually go running on the weekend.

Be careful! The frequency adverb <u>always</u> cannot go before <u>don't</u> or <u>doesn't</u>.
I don't always have breakfast in the morning. NOT I ~~always don't~~ have breakfast in the morning.

Be careful! Don't use <u>never</u> with a negative verb. Use the frequency adverb <u>ever</u>.
I never eat sweets. OR I don't ever eat sweets. NOT I ~~don't never~~ eat sweets.

Time expressions

**Time expressions generally go at the beginning or end of a sentence. When a time expression
is at the beginning, a comma is optional. Don't use a comma when the time expression is at the end.**
Three times a week, I go to the pool.   I go to the pool three times a week.

The time expression <u>a lot</u> goes at the end of a sentence.
I go to the pool a lot. NOT ~~A lot I go to the pool~~.

Some time expressions
every week
every other day
once a month
twice a year
three times a week

Other expressions
once in a while
a lot

B **On a separate sheet of paper, rewrite these sentences correctly.**

1 She plays usually golf on Sunday.

2 They go to the park hardly ever.

3 I always am hungry in the afternoon.

4 We once in a while have eggs for breakfast.

5 Penny doesn't never exercise.

6 Never I go swimming at night.

7 Vivian doesn't drink always coffee.

8 Corey and I play twice a week tennis together.

9 We go often bike riding in the afternoon.

10 She is every day late for class.

UNIT 7 Lesson 1

The past tense of <u>be</u>: form

Use <u>was</u> and <u>were</u> for affirmative statements. Use <u>wasn't</u> and <u>weren't</u> for negative statements.
I was in Rome yesterday.   They were in Paris.
She wasn't on time.   They weren't early.

Begin <u>yes</u> / <u>no</u> questions with <u>Was</u> or <u>Were</u>.
Was your flight late?   Were you late?

Begin information questions with a question word followed by <u>was</u> or <u>were</u>.
How long was your vacation?   How many people were there?
Where was your passport?   Where were your tickets?

A Complete the conversations with <u>was</u>, <u>were</u>, <u>wasn't</u>, or <u>weren't</u>.

1 A: _____ you out of town last week?
   B: No, I _____. Why?
   A: Well, you _____ at work all week.

2 A: How _____ the food?
   B: Great! There _____ lots of fresh seafood
      and the fruit _____ delicious.

3 A: So _____ your vacation OK?
   B: Well, actually it _____. The food _____
      terrible and there _____ too many people.

4 A: Where _____ you last weekend?
   B: I _____ on vacation.
   A: Really? How _____ it?

5 A: How long _____ your trip?
   B: Only a few hours, but we _____ pretty tired.

6 A: _____ your brother on vacation last week?
   B: Yes, he _____. He and his wife _____
      on a cruise.

B On a separate sheet of paper, unscramble the words to write questions, using <u>was</u> or <u>were</u>.

1 your / vacation / very long
2 your luggage / where

3 the drive / comfortable
4 you / on the morning flight

5 your friends / late
6 there / a lot of people / on the train

UNIT 7   Lesson 2

> **The simple past tense: spelling rules for regular verbs**
>
> Form the past tense of most verbs by adding <u>-ed</u> to the base form.
>   play → played
>
> For verbs ending in <u>-e</u> or <u>-ie</u>, add <u>-d</u>.
>   smile → smiled   tie → tied
>
> For one-syllable verbs ending in one vowel + one consonant, double the consonant and add <u>-ed</u>.
>   stop → stopped   plan → planned
>
> For two-syllable verbs ending in one vowel + one consonant: If the first syllable is stressed, add <u>-ed</u>.
>   vi - sit → visited
>
> If the second syllable is stressed, double the consonant and add <u>-ed</u>.
>   pre - fer → preferred
>
> For verbs ending in a consonant and <u>-y</u>, change the <u>-y</u> to <u>-i</u> and add <u>-ed</u>.
>   study → studied
>
> Be careful! Do not use <u>-ed</u> for irregular verbs.
>
> See page 122 for a list of irregular verbs in the simple past tense form.

A On a separate sheet of paper, write the simple past tense form of the following verbs.

1 return _____
2 like _____
3 change _____
4 cry _____

5 try _____
6 stay _____
7 travel _____
8 arrive _____

9 rain _____
10 wait _____
11 offer _____
12 hurry _____

B On a separate sheet of paper, write the simple past tense form of these irregular verbs.

1 eat _____
2 drink _____
3 swim _____
4 go _____

5 write _____
6 meet _____
7 run _____
8 begin _____

9 buy _____
10 read _____
11 pay _____
12 understand _____

The simple past tense: usage and form

Use the simple past tense to talk about completed actions in the past.

My grandparents **went** to Paris in April.

Last year, we **played** tennis and **did** aerobics every day.

Negative forms

Use <u>didn't</u> + the base form of a verb.

He **didn't go** out last weekend. NOT He didn't ~~went~~ out last weekend.

They **didn't have** a good time. NOT They didn't ~~had~~ a good time.

Questions

Begin <u>yes</u> / <u>no</u> questions with <u>Did</u>. Use the base form of the verb.

Did you **go** swimming every day? NOT **Did** you ~~went~~ swimming every day?

Begin information questions with a question word followed by <u>did</u>. Use the base form of the verb.

Where did you **go** shopping?   **When did** he **arrive**?   **What did** they **eat** every day?

C On a separate sheet of paper, change each affirmative statement into a negative statement.

1 I slept all night.

2 We went swimming.

3 She ate a lot of food.

4 They drank a lot of coffee.

5 We had dinner at eight.

6 He bought postcards.

D On a separate sheet of paper, unscramble the words to write questions. Use the simple past tense.

1 you / go / where / on vacation last summer

2 you / from vacation / get back / when

3 they / a good flight / have

4 in London / you / do / what

5 your parents / their trip / enjoy

6 stay / how long / in Paris / Alicia

UNIT 8 Lesson 1

Direct objects: usage

The subject of a sentence performs the action of the verb. A direct object receives the action of the verb.

subject	verb	direct object
I	like	spicy food.
Anne	wears	dark clothes.

A Underline the subjects in the following sentences. Circle the direct objects.

1 <u>Stacey</u> is wearing (a bathrobe) right now.

2 Many people buy outerwear in this store.

3 I love red shoes.

4 Sanford and Gloria never wear shorts.

5 You can't enter this store before 10:00.

6 Do you have your credit card?

7 Marianne wants a pair of warm pajamas.

Indirect objects: usage rules and common errors

When a sentence contains a direct object and a prepositional phrase, you can use an indirect object to say the same thing.

prepositional phrase	indirect object
I'm buying the gloves **for her**.	I'm buying **her** the gloves.
Give the sweater **to Jay**.	Give **Jay** the sweater.

Be careful! When a sentence contains both a direct object and an indirect object, the indirect object always comes first. The direct object CANNOT be a pronoun.

Mindy wrote **her parents** a letter.

Mindy wrote **them** a letter.

NOT Mindy wrote ~~a letter her parents~~.

NOT Mindy wrote ~~a letter them~~.

NOT Mindy wrote her parents ~~it~~.

NOT Mindy wrote them ~~it~~.

B On a separate sheet of paper, rewrite each sentence, changing the prepositional phrase into an indirect object pronoun. Follow the example.

She buys clothes for them. *She buys them clothes.*

1 Laurie sends a check to her father every month.
2 At night we read stories to our children.
3 They serve meals to us in the dining room.
4 They never give gifts to me on my birthday.

C On a separate sheet of paper, rewrite each sentence, changing the indirect object pronoun into a prepositional phrase using the preposition in parentheses. Follow the example.

They never buy me dinner. (for) *They never buy dinner for me.*

1 He always gives me the check. (to)
2 I sent my colleagues the tickets. (to)
3 His friend showed him the check for dinner. (to)
4 She'd like to get her mother a book. (for)

D On a separate sheet of paper, rewrite the following sentences, adding the indirect object or prepositional phrase to each sentence. Don't add any words. Follow the example.

They sent it on Monday. (to me) *They sent it to me on Monday.*

1 Did they give breakfast at the hotel? (you)
2 We always tell the truth. (her)
3 They make lunch every day. (for him)
4 He brought flowers last night. (his wife)

UNIT 8 Lesson 2

Comparative adjectives: spelling rules

Add -er to one-syllable adjectives. If the adjective ends in -e, add -r.
tight → tighter   loose → looser

If an adjective ends in a consonant-vowel-consonant sequence, double the final consonant before adding -er.
hot → hotter

For most adjectives that end in -y, change the y to i and add -er.
pretty → prettier   busy → busier

To make the comparative form of most adjectives that have more than two syllables, use more or less.
affordable → more affordable   convenient → less convenient

When comparing two things that are both in the sentence, use than before the second thing.
She's less practical than her sister.   The weather is warmer there than here.

A On a separate sheet of paper, write the comparative form of the following adjectives.

1 tall	5 light	9 sad	13 spicy	17 popular
2 sunny	6 clean	10 fatty	14 healthy	18 red
3 comfortable	7 bad	11 salty	15 cute	19 conservative
4 heavy	8 late	12 sweet	16 short	20 interesting

B Complete each sentence with a comparative adjective. Use **than** if necessary.

1 I like the pink purse. It's much _____ (nice).
2 Low-fat milk is not bad, but no-fat milk is _____ (good).
3 France is _____ (small) Russia.
4 Women's shoes are usually _____ (expensive) men's shoes.
5 It's hot during the day, but it's _____ (cool) at night.
6 He's a lot _____ (tall) his brother.
7 This projector is a lot _____ (popular), but it's _____ (affordable).
8 They're much _____ (liberal) about clothing rules at the beach.
9 It's usually _____ (sunny) in the morning before the rain begins.
10 French fries are _____ (fatty) and _____ (salty) a salad.

Modals *can*, *could*, and *should*: meaning, form, and common errors

Meaning
Use <u>can</u> to express ability or possibility.
Jerome can speak Korean.   I can be there before 8:00.

Use <u>could</u> to suggest an alternative or to make a weak suggestion.
They could see an old movie like *Titanic*, or they could go to something new.
You could eat a healthier diet.

Use <u>should</u> to give advice or to express criticism.
You should think before you speak.

Form
Modals are followed by the base form of the main verb of the sentence, except in short answers to questions.
You can eat at a lot of good restaurants in this neighborhood.
Who should read this? They should.
Can you see the moon tonight? Yes, I can.

Use <u>not</u> between the modal and the base form.
You shouldn't stay at the Galaxy Hotel.   They can't take the express.

In <u>yes</u> / <u>no</u> questions, the modal precedes the subject of the sentence. In information questions, the question word precedes the modal.

Yes / <u>no</u> questions	**Information questions**
Should I buy a round-trip ticket?	When should they leave?
Can we make the 1:05 flight?	Why should they go?
Could she take an express train?	Which trains could I take?
	Who could they call?

> **BUT: Note the word order when <u>Who</u> is the subject.**
>
> Who can give me the information?
> (The travel agent can.)

Common errors
Never add <u>-s</u> to the third-person singular form of modals.
He should buy a ticket in advance. NOT ~~He shoulds buy~~ a ticket in advance.

Never use <u>to</u> between modals and the base form.
You could take the train or the bus. NOT You ~~could to take~~ the train or the bus.

Circle the correct phrases to complete the sentences.

1 Who (should buy / should to buy) the tickets?

2 Where (I can find / can I find) a hotel?

3 You (could to walk / could walk) or (take / taking) the bus.

4 (I should to call / Should I call) you when I arrive?

5 We (can to not take / can't take) the bus; it left.

6 When (should you giving / should you give) the agent your boarding pass?

7 Which trains (can get / can getting) me there soon?

Expansion: future actions

There are four ways to express future actions, using present forms.

<u>Be going to</u>
<u>Be going to</u> + base form usually expresses a future plan or certain knowledge about the future.
I'm going to spend my summer in Africa.   She's going to get a rental car when she arrives.
It's going to rain tomorrow.

The present continuous
The present continuous can also express a future plan.
We're traveling tonight.   We aren't wearing formal clothes to the wedding.
We aren't eating at home tomorrow.

The simple present tense

The simple present tense can express a future action, especially with verbs of motion: <u>arrive</u>, <u>come</u>, <u>depart</u>, <u>fly</u>, <u>go</u>, <u>leave</u>, <u>sail</u>, and <u>start</u>—especially when on a schedule or a timetable. When the simple present tense expresses the future, there is almost always a word, phrase, or clause indicating the future time.

This Monday, the express leaves at noon.   The flight arrives at 9:00 tonight.

The present of <u>be</u>

The present of <u>be</u> can describe a future event if it includes a word or phrase that indicates the future.

The wedding is on Sunday.

A Read the arrival and departure schedules. Then complete each sentence or question with the simple present tense.

1 The bus _____ at 11:00. It _____ at 8:00.

2 When _____ the flight _____?
It _____ at 23:30.

3 What time _____ the train _____ in Beijing? At 10:20 P.M.

4 _____ the train _____ at 7:00? Yes, it does.

B On a separate sheet of paper, answer each of the following questions with a complete sentence. There may be more than one correct way to answer each question.

1 What are your plans for your next vacation?

2 What are you going to do this weekend?

3 What are you doing this evening?

UNIT 10   Lesson 1

Comparative and superlative adjectives: usage and form

Usage

Comparative adjectives compare two people, places, or things. Use <u>than</u> if the second item is mentioned right after the adjective.

Mexico City is larger than Los Angeles.   Housing in New York is more expensive than in Lima.

Compared with Los Angeles, Mexico City is larger.   Compared with Lima, housing is more expensive in New York.

Superlative adjectives compare more than two people, places, or things.

Compared to other cities in the Americas, Mexico City is the largest.

> Be careful! **Use <u>the</u> with superlative adjectives.**
> Don't say: Mexico City is ~~largest~~.

Form

adjective	comparative adjective	superlative adjective
cheap	cheaper (than)	the cheapest
expensive	more expensive (than)	the most expensive
practical	less practical (than)	the least practical

Superlative adjectives: spelling

Add <u>-est</u> to one-syllable adjectives. If the adjective ends in <u>-e</u>, add <u>-st</u>.

cheap → the cheapest   loose → the loosest

If an adjective ends in a consonant-vowel-consonant sequence, double the final consonant before adding <u>-est</u>.

hot → the hottest

For most adjectives that end in <u>-y</u>, change the y to <u>i</u> and add <u>-est</u>.

pretty → the prettiest   busy → the busiest

To form the superlative of most adjectives of two or more syllables, use <u>the most</u> or <u>the least</u>.

Car trips are the least expensive vacations.   Cruises are the most relaxing vacations.

A Write <u>both</u> the comparative and superlative form of each of the following adjectives.

		comparative	superlative			comparative	superlative
1	tall	_____	_____	10	interesting	_____	_____
2	easy	_____	_____	11	conservative	_____	_____
3	liberal	_____	_____	12	light	_____	_____
4	heavy	_____	_____	13	casual	_____	_____
5	unusual	_____	_____	14	comfortable	_____	_____
6	pretty	_____	_____	15	relaxing	_____	_____
7	exciting	_____	_____	16	long	_____	_____
8	wild	_____	_____	17	short	_____	_____
9	informal	_____	_____	18	scary	_____	_____

B Complete each sentence with a comparative or superlative adjective. Use <u>than</u> if necessary.

1 That dinner was _____ (delicious) meal we had on our vacation.

2 This scanner is definitely _____ (good) other one.

3 The Caribbean cruise is _____ (relaxing) of our vacation packages.

4 The Honsu X24 is a good camera, but the Cashio is _____ (easy) to use.

5 We have several brands, but I'd say the R300 is _____ (popular).

6 Sunday was _____ (bad) day of our vacation.

7 I like that rug, but I think this one is _____ (beautiful).

8 Our vacation in Brazil was _____ (nice) our vacation in Italy last year.

9 There are so many brands to choose from. Which brand is _____ (good)?

10 All three cameras look good. But which one is _____ (easy) to use?

11 I like both the J12 and the Pro MP3 players, but which one's _____ (small)?

12 Which of these three plates do you think is _____ (pretty)?

13 I can't decide if I should read this book or that one. Which one is _____ (interesting)?

UNIT 10   Lesson 2

Intensifiers <u>very</u>, <u>really</u>, and <u>too</u>

Intensifiers make the meaning of adjectives stronger.

<u>Very</u> and <u>really</u> have the same meaning. They can intensify adjectives with a positive or negative meaning.
> That restaurant is **really** (or **very**) **good**. I want to go there.
> That movie is **really** (or **very**) **scary**. I don't want to see it.

<u>Too</u> also makes the meaning of adjectives stronger. But <u>too</u> expresses the idea of "more than enough."
<u>Too</u> usually has a negative meaning.
> That movie is **too long**. I don't want to see it.
> This restaurant is **too expensive**. I'm not going to eat here.

Be careful! Don't use <u>too</u> to intensify adjectives with a positive meaning. Use <u>very</u> and <u>really</u>.
> This camera is **very** affordable! NOT This camera is ~~too affordable~~!

A Complete each sentence with <u>too</u>, <u>really</u>, or <u>very</u> and your own adjective.

1 Beach vacations are _____. I love them.

2 French fries are _____. You shouldn't eat them every day.

3 A cruise is _____. I don't have enough money to take one.

4 They say this movie is _____. I want to see it.

5 This book is _____. You should read it.

6 English is _____. People are learning it all over the world.

7 This printer is _____. I need to replace it.

8 These pants are _____. I need to buy a larger pair.

B Complete each conversation, using <u>too</u> or <u>enough</u>.

1 A: How about this? Should we buy it for your mother?
   B: No. It isn't _____ (pretty). I want something nicer.

2 A: Do you think this rug is too small?
   B: No, it's great. I think it's _____ (big).

3 A: Did you buy a microwave yesterday?
   B: I looked at some. But they were _____ (expensive).

4 A: Why are you sending that steak back to the chef?
   B: It's an expensive meal, and this steak just isn't _____ (good).

5 A: You never eat dessert?
   B: No. Desserts are _____ (sweet) for me.

6 A: How was your vacation?
   B: To tell the truth, it just wasn't _____ (relaxing).

7 A: How's that soup? Is it _____ (hot)?
   B: No, it's fine. Thanks.

8 A: Would you like more ice in your water?
   B: Yes, please. It isn't _____ (cold).

TOP NOTCH
1B
Writing Booster

Writing Booster

The Writing Booster is optional. It is intended to teach students the conventions of written English. Each unit's Writing Booster is focused both on a skill and its application to the Writing Exercise from the Unit Review page.

UNIT 6 *Punctuation of statements and questions*

Use a period at the end of a statement.
I go to the gym every morning.

Use a question mark at the end of a question.
What do you do to stay in shape?

Use an exclamation point at the end of a sentence if you want to indicate that something is funny or surprising.
The truth is I'm a couch potato!

> . (a period)
> ? (a question mark)
> ! (an exclamation point)
> , (a comma)
> **Remember:**
> **Use commas to connect more than two ideas in a series.**
> I go to the gym, run in the park, and go bike riding every weekend.

A Rewrite each statement or question, using correct punctuation. Remember to begin each with a capital letter.

1 she doesn't have time to exercise
2 do you get enough sleep every night
3 my friends think I exercise a lot but I don't
4 we go running bike riding and swimming in the summer

5 my father never eats sweets
6 what do you do on weekends
7 they eat junk food watch TV and stay up late every night
8 are you a couch potato

B Guidance for Writing (page 72) Use the ideas as a guide to help you write six questions about fitness and eating habits for your interview.

> **Ideas**
> • favorite activities
> • exercise routines
> • foods you eat
> • foods you avoid
> • what you can or can't do

UNIT 7 *Time order*

Use a time clause in a sentence to show the order of events.
We visited the old part of town after we had lunch.
We checked into our hotel before we had lunch.

You can begin a sentence with a time clause. Most writers use a comma when the time clause comes first.
After we had lunch, we visited the old part of town.
Before we had lunch, we checked into our hotel

Use transition signals to show time order in a paragraph. Use <u>First</u> to begin a series and <u>Finally</u> to end one. Use <u>Then</u>, <u>Next</u>, and <u>After that</u> to indicate a series of events. Commas are optional.
First, we checked in to our hotel. After we had lunch, we visited the old part of town and took pictures. Then, we went to the beach and lay in the sun for a while. Next, we played golf. After that, we went shopping and bought a rug. Finally, we went back to our hotel.

A On a separate sheet of paper, use the cues to write sentences. Begin each sentence with a time clause. Follow the example.

(before) First we had lunch. Then we went to the beach. *Before we went to the beach, we had lunch.*

1 (after) First we visited Rome. Then we went to Venice.
2 (before) First they went snorkeling. After that, they had lunch.
3 (after) He arrived in Miami on Saturday. Then he looked for a hotel.

4 (before) I spent three days in Mexico City. Next I flew to Cancún.
5 (after) She got back from the airport. After that, she called her mother.
6 (before) The weather was beautiful. Then it rained.

B On a separate sheet of paper, rewrite the paragraph, using time-order transition words.

> Let me tell you about my trip. I flew from New York to London. It was very interesting, and I spent two days there. I took the train through the Chunnel to Paris. Paris was amazing. I got a car and drove to Rome. It was a long drive, but it was really scenic. I took a boat to the island of Sardinia. It was very beautiful. I flew back to London and back home to New York.

C **Guidance for Writing (page 84)** Write sentences describing your vacation in the order that the events happened. Then use them to write your paragraph, using time clauses and time-order transition words.

UNIT 8 *Connecting ideas with <u>because</u> and <u>since</u>*

Clauses with <u>because</u> and <u>since</u> present reasons. There's no difference in meaning between <u>because</u> and <u>since</u> in the following sentences.
> I'm going to Paris because I love French food.
> He's not wearing a jacket since he left it in the restaurant.

In speaking, it's OK to answer a question using just a clause with <u>because</u> or <u>since</u>.
> A: Why are you wearing jeans?
> B: Because it's a really casual restaurant.

In writing, however, a clause beginning with <u>because</u> or <u>since</u> is not a sentence; it's an incomplete thought. Connect the clause beginning with <u>because</u> or <u>since</u> to a sentence to make the thought complete.
> I wear jeans at that restaurant because it is a really casual restaurant.

Remember:
In English, a sentence is a group of words containing a subject and a verb. It expresses a complete thought.

A clause with <u>because</u> or <u>since</u> can come at the beginning or the end of the sentence. When it comes at the beginning, use a comma. It's good writing style to vary placement so all sentences don't sound the same.
> I eat vegetables every day because they are healthy.
> Because they are healthy, I eat vegetables every day.

A On a separate sheet of paper, connect the sentences, using clauses with either <u>because</u> or <u>since</u>. Be careful! make sure the clause with <u>because</u> or <u>since</u> presents a reason.

1 I'm wearing a sweater. I feel cold.

2 She called her brother. It was his birthday.

3 He bought a blue blazer. He needed it for a business trip.

4 They didn't have a ticket for the concert. They stayed home.

5 Our DVD player is broken. We have to get a new one.

B On a separate sheet of paper, answer each of the following questions with a complete sentence containing a clause with <u>because</u> or <u>since</u>. Follow the example.

Why do you like classical music?   *I like classical music because it is happy music.*

1 Why are you studying English?

2 Why is a clothes store better than a clothes website?

3 Why do people like malls?

4 Why are running shoes more comfortable than formal shoes?

C **Guidance for Writing (page 96)** Write a list of at least five clothing do's and don'ts for appropriate dress in your country. Explain the reasons for the tips, using <u>because</u> and <u>since</u>. Use your sentences as a guide to help you write your letter or e-mail.

Don't wear jeans to nice restaurants because people think they're inappropriate.

A paragraph is a group of sentences that relate to a topic or a theme. When your writing contains information about a variety of topics, it is convenient to divide your writing into separate paragraphs.

Traditionally, **the first word of a paragraph is indented.** (Sometimes new paragraphs, especially in books, are not indented. Instead, a separation is made by leaving a blank line space as below.)

In the writing model to the right, the first paragraph is about Holland and the second is about Thailand. Dividing the writing into two paragraphs makes it easier to read and understand.

Clothing customs in different countries

Holland has a northern climate, so depending on the time of year you're visiting, pack lighter or heavier clothes. One thing people notice about Holland is the way young people dress. Their dress code is "anything goes," so it's not unusual to see some pretty wild clothes there.

On the other hand, if you're visiting Thailand from May to September, pack for the heat. Thailand is generally conservative when it comes to clothing, but at Thailand's magnificent temples, the rules about clothing, and especially shoes, are very strict. If your shoes are too open, they are considered disrespectful, and you will have to change to more modest ones. So be prepared with light but modest clothing and shoes for your Thailand trip.

A Write a check mark ✔ in the place or places where a new paragraph could or should start. Then, on a separate sheet of paper, copy the paragraphs, indenting each one.

Famous families

Jackie Chan is a movie star and singer from Hong Kong. His wife, Joan Lin, is an actress from Taiwan. They have a son, JC Chan. He's a student in the United States. Another famous family is the Williams family. Venus and Serena Williams are famous tennis players. Their mother's name is Oracene Price. Their father, Richard Williams, is their manager. Still another famous family is the Fernández family from Mexico. Vicente and Alejandro are father and son. They are both singers, and they are famous all over Latin America.

B Guidance for Writing (page 108) **Use your answers to the questions below as a guide to help you write your paragraphs.**

Paragraph 1

Begin your paragraph with an opening statement, such as: Last month, I went to ___ .

- Where did you go?
- What kind of transportation did you take?
- When did you leave?
- Who did you travel with?
- What did you do when you were there?
- When did you get back?

Paragraph 2

Begin your next paragraph with an opening statement, such as: On my next trip, . . .

- Where are you going to go?
- What kind of transportation are you going to take?
- When are you leaving?
- Who are you traveling with?
- What are you going to do when you are there?
- When are you getting back?

Use <u>even though</u> to connect contradictory ideas in a sentence. (A comma is optional before <u>even though</u> when it comes at the end of the sentence.)

Bee Flowers is the most popular shop in town even though it's quite expensive.
You can bargain for really low prices at Marty's, even though the service isn't very friendly.

Always use a comma if the clause that begins with <u>even though</u> comes first.

Even though it's quite expensive, Bee Flowers is the most popular shop in town.
Even though the service isn't very friendly, you can bargain for really low prices at Marty's.

Use <u>however</u> and <u>on the other hand</u> at the beginning of a sentence to connect contradictory ideas from one sentence to another. Use a comma.

You can bargain for really low prices at Marty's. However, the service isn't very friendly.
Bee Flowers is quite expensive. On the other hand, it's the most popular shop in town.

Be careful! Don't use <u>however</u> or <u>on the other hand</u> to combine clauses in a sentence.

Don't write: You can bargain for really low prices at Marty's, ~~however the service isn't very friendly.~~

A **On a separate sheet of paper, combine each pair of sentences into one sentence, using <u>even though</u>. Then rewrite your sentences, using <u>even though</u> to begin each one.**

1 You can find some good deals at the Savoy Hotel. Their rooms are the most expensive in town.

2 You can bargain for really low prices at the Old Market. It isn't the prettiest place to shop.

3 The Philcov X30 is easy to use and not too expensive. It isn't the most popular camera.

4 The prices of flat screen TVs are getting lower every year. They can still be very expensive.

5 The Samson camcorder is the most professional camera you can buy. It isn't the lightest.

B **Now, on a separate sheet of paper, write the sentences again, using <u>however</u> or <u>on the other hand</u>.**

C Guidance for Writing (page 120) **Write at least six sentences about places to shop in your town or city. Use <u>even though</u>, <u>however</u>, and <u>on the other hand</u>. Use your sentences as a guide to help you write your guide.**

Top Notch Pop Lyrics

1:15/1:16
🔊 It's Nice To Meet You   [Unit 1]
(CHORUS)
It's nice to meet you.
Good to meet you.
Pleasure to meet you.

What's your name?
My name is Mr. Johnson.
Please just call me Stan.
I'd like you to meet my wife, Mary Anne.

(CHORUS)

What do you do?
Actually, I'm a teacher
at the Children's Institute.
The little kids are really cute.
That sounds nice. Where are you from—
somewhere far or near?
As a matter of fact, Chicago is my
hometown.
Could you say that louder please?
How did you end up here?
My father was a salesman.
We moved all around.

(CHORUS)

Who is that?
Let me introduce you
to my new friend Eileen.
She's a chef and she's nineteen.

(CHORUS)

Good-bye. Take care.

1:34/1:35
🔊 Going Out   [Unit 2]
Do you want to see a play?
What time does the play begin?
It starts at eight. Is that OK?
I'd love to go. I'll see you then.
I heard it got some good reviews.
Where's it playing? What's the show?
It's called "One Single Life to Lose."
I'll think about it. I don't know.

(CHORUS)
Everything will be all right
when you and I go out tonight.

When Thomas Soben gives his talk—
The famous chef? That's not for me!
The doors open at nine o'clock.
There's a movie we could see
at Smith and Second Avenue.
That's my favorite neighborhood!
I can't wait to be with you.
I can't wait to have some food.

(CHORUS)

We're going to have a good time.
Don't keep me up past my bedtime.
We'll make a date.
Tonight's the night.
It starts at eight.
The price is right!
I'm a fan of pop.

Classical is more my style.
I like blues and I like soul.
Bach and Mozart make me smile!
Around the corner and down the street.
That's the entrance to the park.
There's a place where we could meet.
I wouldn't go there after dark!

(CHORUS: 2 times)

2:18/2:19
🔊 An Only Child   [Unit 3]
Let me see the photos of
your wife and family.
Who's that guy there, on the right,
next to the TV?
Is that your younger brother, John?
And who are those two?
Your sisters both look so alike.
Please tell me what they do.

(CHORUS)
I ask so many questions.
You just answer with a smile.
You have a large family,
but I am an only child.

How about your cousins now?
Please tell me something new.
Do they both play basketball?
You know that I do, too.

(CHORUS)

I don't have a brother,
but you have two or three.
You're all one big happy family.
I don't have a sister,
but you have older twins.
This is a game I can't ever win.
Do you have nieces and nephews,
and how many are there now?
Do they all like the same kinds of things?
Are they different somehow?

(CHORUS)

2:34/2:35
🔊 The World Café   [Unit 4]
Is there something that you want?
Is there anything you need?
Have you made up your mind
what you want to eat?
Place your order now,
or do you need more time?
Why not start with some juice—
lemon, orange, or lime?
Some like it hot, some like it sweet,
some like it really spicy.
You may not like everything you eat,
but I think we're doing nicely.

(CHORUS)
I can understand every word you say.
Tonight we're speaking English at
The World Café.

I'll take the main course now.
I think I'll have the fish.

Does it come with the choice of another
dish?
Excuse me waiter, please—
I think I'm in the mood
for a little dessert, and the cake looks good.
Do you know? Are there any low-fat desserts
that we could try now?
I feel like having a bowl of fruit.
Do you have to say good-bye now?

(CHORUS)

Apples, oranges, cheese, and ham,
coffee, juice, milk, bread, and jam,
rice and beans, meat and potatoes,
eggs and ice cream,
grilled tomatoes—
That's the menu.
That's the list.
Is there anything I missed?

(CHORUS)

3:22/3:23
🔊 It's Not Working Again   [Unit 5]
Hi. I'm calling on my cell phone.
I need a little help with a fax machine.
It's not working, and it's pretty bad.
I feel like I've been had, if you know
what I mean.
I'm coming to the store right now.
Can you show me how to use it?
The front lid won't open.
When my cat's around,
it squeaks and makes a funny sound.

(CHORUS)
It's not working again.
It's driving me crazy.
It's not working again.

I called yesterday, and a guy named Jack
said,
"I'm busy right now, can I call you back?"
He didn't even ask me what was wrong
with it.
He didn't want to hear the short and
long of it.
I just bought the thing yesterday,
and it won't turn on so please don't say,
"I'm sorry to hear that.
That's a shame.
That's too bad."
It's all a game.

(CHORUS)

I'm not looking for a laptop computer
or an X340 or a PDA.
Just tell me what's wrong with my fax
machine
so I can say good-bye and be on my way.
It won't send a copy of my document.
The paper goes through, and it comes
out bent.
On second thought, it's guaranteed.
I want my money back—that's what I need.

(CHORUS: 2 times)

A Typical Day [Unit 6]

The Couch Potato sits around.
He eats junk food by the pound.
It's just a typical day.
Watching as the world goes by,
he's out of shape and wonders why.
It's just a typical day.

(CHORUS)
Every night he dreams that he's
skydiving through the air.
And sometimes you appear.
He says, "What are you doing here?"

He cleans the house and plays guitar,
takes a shower, drives the car.
It's just a typical day.
He watches TV all alone,
reads and sleeps, talks on the phone.
It's just a typical day.

(CHORUS)

I'm sorry.
Mr. Couch Potato's resting right now.
Can he call you back?
He usually lies down every day of the week,
and he always has to have a snack.
Now all his dreams are coming true.
He's making plans to be with you.
It's just a typical day.
He goes walking once a week.
He's at the theater as we speak!
It's just a typical day.

(CHORUS)

My Dream Vacation [Unit 7]

The ride was bumpy
and much too long.
It was pretty boring.
It felt so wrong.
I slept all night,
and it rained all day.
We left the road,
and we lost the way.
Then you came along
and you took my hand.
You whispered words
I could understand.

(CHORUS)
On my dream vacation,
I dream of you.
I don't ever want to wake up.
On my dream vacation,
this much is true:
I don't ever want it to stop.

The food was awful.
They stole my purse.
The whole two weeks went
from bad to worse.
They canceled my ticket.
I missed my flight.
They were so unfriendly
it just wasn't right.
So I called a taxi,
and I got inside,

and there you were,
sitting by my side.

(CHORUS)

You were so unusual.
The day was so exciting.
I opened up my eyes,
and you were gone.
I waited for hours.
You never called.
I watched TV
and looked at the walls.
Where did you go to?
Why weren't you near?
Did you have a reason
to disappear?
So I flew a plane
to the south of France,
and I heard you say,
Would you like to play?"

(CHORUS)

Anything Goes [Unit 8]

The shoe department's upstairs.
It's on the second floor.
Women's Casual is down the stairs,
there by the door.
This helpful store directory
shows every kind of clothes.
I look for the department where
it says anything goes.

(CHORUS)
At home and when I travel,
I always like to wear
pajamas in the daytime
with a blazer and a pair
of socks on my fingers
and gloves on my toes—
anything goes.

On the ground floor, there's a restaurant
and a photo studio,
so I take the escalator
down to the floor below.
There are turtlenecks and T-shirts.
There are cardigans and jeans
in every size and color.
They look comfortable and clean.

(CHORUS)

The salesperson says,
"Here you go.
Try it on.
That's not too bad.
Let me see if I can find you something
better."
Some people say that black clothes
are more flattering than white,
or they think that they look nicer
in the day or in the night.
Their clothes can't be too liberal
or too conservative.
If I love it, then I wear it.
That's the way I want to live.

(CHORUS)

Five Hundred Ways [Unit 9]

You could take the bus,
or you could take the train.
You could take the ferry,
or you could take a plane.
Baby, it's a small world,
when all is said and done.
We have so many options,
the question is, which one?

(CHORUS)
There are five hundred ways to get here.
What are you going to do?
You could get a one-way ticket to see me.
I'm waiting here for you.

You should really hurry.
When are you going to call
and make your reservation?
You could miss them all.
And do you know how long
you are going to stay?
You could come and be with me
forever and a day.

(CHORUS)

Follow me.
Follow me.
Yes, you can follow me.
You have my phone number,
and you have my address.
Tell me, are you coming on
the local or express?

(CHORUS)

Shopping for Souvenirs [Unit 10]

I go to the bank at a quarter to ten.
I pick up my cash from the ATM.
Here at the store, it won't be too hard
to take out a check or a credit card.
The bank has a good rate of exchange,
and everything here is in my price range.
The easiest part of this bargain hunt
is that I can afford anything I want.

(CHORUS)
Whenever I travel around the world,
I spend my money for two.
Shopping for souvenirs
helps me to be near you.

I try to decide how much I should pay
for the beautiful art I see on display.
To get a great deal, I can't be too nice.
It can't hurt to ask for a better price.

(CHORUS)

Yes, it's gorgeous, and I love it.
It's the biggest and the best,
though it might not be the cheapest.
How much is it—more than all the rest?
I'll pass on some good advice to you:
When you're in Rome, do as the Romans do.
A ten percent tip for the taxi fare
should be good enough when you're staying
there.

(CHORUS)

SECOND EDITION

TOP NOTCH
1B

Workbook

Joan Saslow • Allen Ascher

With Barbara R. Denman and Julie C. Rouse

PEARSON
Longman

Staying in Shape

1 **Look at the pictures. Name each activity. Write the letter on the line.**

Ⓐ Ⓑ Ⓒ Ⓓ Ⓔ Ⓕ Ⓖ Ⓗ Ⓘ

_____ **1.** swimming   _____ **4.** shooting   _____ **7.** running

_____ **2.** walking   _____ **5.** playing soccer   _____ **8.** lifting weights

_____ **3.** doing aerobics   _____ **6.** cooking dinner   _____ **9.** sleeping

2 **Choose the correct response. Write the letter on the line.**

1. Kate has music class on Mondays. She goes to class _____.   **a.** once in a while

2. The first thing I do in the morning is drink coffee. I drink coffee _____.   **b.** every weekend

3. I play basketball, but not as much as I'd like to. I play _____.   **c.** never

4. Anna's husband does all the cooking. Anna _____ cooks.   **d.** every day

5. Jim and Dean always play golf on Saturday or Sunday. They play golf _____.   **e.** once a week

3 **How often do you do these activities? Complete the chart.**

Activity	How often?
ride a bike	
eat in a restaurant	
shop for clothes	
shop for food	
watch TV	
clean your house	
exercise	

4 **Answer the questions. Use your own words.**

1. "What are you up to?"

YOU _____

2. "Are you in shape or out of shape?"

YOU _____

3. "What are you crazy about?"

YOU _____

5 **Complete the sentences. Use <u>have to</u> or <u>has to</u>.**

1. I _____ go to class this morning. Do you have my textbook?

2. She can sleep late tomorrow. She doesn't _____ work until 10:30.

3. My brother isn't healthy. He _____ exercise more.

4. They don't _____ pick us up at the train station. We can take a taxi.

5. Pete _____ buy a new digital camera. His old one isn't working.

6. Do you _____ work next Saturday?

7. We _____ finish our report before the next sales meeting.

6 **Write sentences. Use words from each box.**

| I
My parents
My teacher
My friend
My boss
My brother | **+** | has to
don't have to
can
can't
have to
doesn't have to | **+** | work late on Friday.
play tennis this weekend.
go to school.
study English.
go shopping this weekend.
cook dinner tonight.
sleep late tomorrow morning. |

1. _My brother doesn't have to study English._ _____

2. _____

3. _____

4. _____

5. _____

7 **Look at the responses. Write questions with <u>can</u> or <u>have to</u>.**

1. **A:** (Gail / speak Polish) _Can Gail speak Polish_ _____?
   B: No. She speaks English and French.

2. **A:** (you / play basketball tonight) _____?
   B: Sure. I'm not busy.

3. **A:** (you / meet your brother at the airport) _____?
   B: No, I don't. He's taking a bus.

4. **A:** (I / call you tomorrow) _____?
   B: OK. That would be great.

5. **A:** (Frank / buy a new printer) _____?
   B: No. He fixed his old one.

6. **A:** (they / take the exam on Friday) _____?
   B: Yes, they do. They're studying tonight.

8 Look at Paula's daily planner. Answer the questions about her schedule.

1. Can Paula go running Saturday morning at 9:00?
   No, she can't. She has to study English.

2. What does Paula have to do on Sunday afternoon?
   _____

3. Does Paula have to work on Friday?
   _____

4. Why can't Paula do aerobics Sunday night at 7:30?
   _____

5. Can Paula sleep late on Sunday morning?
   _____

Daily Planner

	FRIDAY	SATURDAY	SUNDAY
9:00	Arrive at the office	English class	
11:00			
1:00	Sales meeting	Lunch with Dad	Clean the house
3:00			
5:00	Leave the office	Shop for a new cell phone	Cook dinner
7:00	Do aerobics		See a movie with Sara

9 Choose the correct response. Circle the letter.

1. "Why don't we go bike riding this weekend?"
   a. Too bad.   b. Sounds good.   c. Don't bother.

2. "I'd love to go fishing with you sometime."
   a. When's good for you?   b. Want to come along?   c. What are you up to?

3. "When's good for you?"
   a. Sorry, I can't.   b. How about Thursday?   c. Once a week.

4. "Saturday at noon is perfect."
   a. I'm sorry to hear that.   b. Well, how about Sunday?   c. Great. See you then.

LESSON 2

10 Complete the sentences with places from the box.

gym	athletic field	pool	court	track	course

1. The school _____ is used for a lot of different sports. Students play football and soccer in the fall and baseball in the spring.

2. You can take an aerobics class or use exercise machines at a _____.

3. The hotel has a tennis _____ and an 18-hole golf _____.

4. On Fridays, there are water aerobics classes in the swimming _____.

5. You can go running or walking on a _____.

11 Look at Dave's activity schedule for September. Then complete the sentences. Circle the letter.

Dave's Activity Schedule ## September

Sunday	Monday	Tuesday	Wednesday	Thursday	Friday	Saturday
	1 lift weights at the gym 5:30 PM	**2**	**3** play basketball 7:00 PM	**4** lift weights at the gym 5:30 PM	**5** study English 8:45 PM	**6** lift weights at the gym 5:30 PM
7 clean the house 10:00 AM	**8** lift weights at the gym 5:30 PM	**9** lift weights at the gym 5:30 PM	**10** play basketball 7:00 PM	**11** lift weights at the gym 5:30 PM	**12** study English 8:45 PM	**13** go running at the track 12:00 PM
14 clean the house 10:00 AM	**15** go running at the track 7:00 PM	**16** lift weights at the gym 5:30 PM	**17** play basketball 7:00 PM	**18** lift weights at the gym 5:30 PM	**19**	**20** lift weights at the gym 10:00 AM play golf 3:00 PM
21 clean the house 10:00 AM lift weights at the gym 1:00 PM	**22** lift weights at the gym 5:30 PM	**23** lift weights at the gym 5:30 PM	**24** play basketball 7:00 PM	**25** lift weights at the gym 5:30 PM	**26** study English 8:45 PM	**27** go bike riding 5:00 PM
28 clean the house 10:00 AM	**29** lift weights at the gym 5:30 PM	**30**				

1. Dave _____ goes bike riding.
   a. hardly ever
   b. never
   c. always

2. Dave _____ cleans the house on Sundays.
   a. always
   b. sometimes
   c. never

3. Dave lifts weights _____.
   a. once a week
   b. at least three times a week
   c. once in a while

4. Dave plays basketball _____.
   a. on Tuesdays
   b. on Wednesdays
   c. on weekends

5. Dave usually lifts weights _____.
   a. in the evening
   b. in the morning
   c. in the afternoon

6. Dave goes running _____.
   a. once a month
   b. every weekend
   c. once in a while

12 Write sentences about your own activities.

Examples: *I occasionally eat in a restaurant.*

I ride a bike once in a while.

1. _____

2. _____

3. _____

4. _____

5. _____

13 Look at the responses. Complete the questions. Use the simple present tense.

1. **A:** How often *does Jim play tennis* _____?

   B: Jim hardly ever plays tennis.

2. **A:** How often _____?

   B: I go walking every day.

3. **A:** When _____?

   B: I usually cook dinner at 7:00.

4. **A:** When _____?

   B: They go jogging on Friday nights.

5. **A:** Where _____?

   B: We do aerobics at the gym.

6. **A:** Where _____?

   B: Kyle plays soccer at the athletic field.

14 Write sentences. Use the simple present tense or the present continuous.

1. Charlie / usually / play golf / on weekends

   Charlie usually plays golf on weekends. _____

2. Adam / talk on the phone / right now

   _____

3. My stepbrother / hardly ever / clean the house

   _____

4. We / go jogging / tonight

   _____

5. I / sleep late / tomorrow morning

   _____

6. Cindy / go swimming / twice a week

   _____

7. Deanna / almost always / watch TV / on weeknights

   _____

8. They / work late / next Tuesday

   _____

15 Choose the correct response. Write the letter on the line.

_____ 1. "How often do you do aerobics?"

_____ 2. "Where are you off to?"

_____ 3. "How often do you go swimming?"

_____ 4. "When do you go fishing?"

_____ 5. "How come you're not going running tonight?"

_____ 6. "Are you studying right now?"

a. Because I'm too busy.

b. No, I'm not. I'm watching TV.

c. I go to the gym once a week.

d. I hardly ever go to the pool.

e. On Fridays.

f. I'm meeting my sister at the pool in 15 minutes.

LESSONS 3 and 4

16 Read the letters to a health magazine advice column.

Dear In-Shape,

I have two health questions for you. I'm an athlete. I play baseball for my university team and I go running every day. I exercise all the time. I think I'm in terrific shape, but I'm worried that I exercise too much. That's my first question—how much exercise is too much?

My second question is about my diet. I try to eat healthy. I hardly ever eat pizza, fast food, or other snacks. I never drink soft drinks. But I have one really bad habit: I have a sweet tooth! I eat too much chocolate, candy, cake, and ice cream. How can I cut down on sweets?

—Ron Miller

Dear In-Shape,

I need some exercise advice! I don't feel very healthy. I get tired just walking from my house to my car! My doctor said that I have to exercise more. I'm sure that she's right. I should get out of the house more often. My husband goes running every day, but I never go running with him. I'm a couch potato. My big activity is watching movies—I watch a movie just about every night. Unfortunately, you don't burn many calories watching TV!

By the way, the problem is not my diet. I generally try to eat foods that are good for me, like fish, vegetables, and fruit. I avoid snacks and I almost never eat sweets!

—Nina Hunter

Now read the letters again. Complete the chart about Ron's and Nina's diet and exercise habits. Check the boxes.

	Ron Miller	Nina Hunter
is in shape	☐	☐
is out of shape	☐	☐
eats junk food	☐	☐
avoids sweets	☐	☐
is crazy about sweets	☐	☐

17 **Read the sentences about Ron and Nina. Check true, false, or no information.**

	true	false	no information
1. Ron doesn't have time to exercise.	☐	☐	☐
2. Ron generally avoids junk food.	☐	☐	☐
3. Ron usually drinks a lot of water.	☐	☐	☐
4. Nina never eats fish.	☐	☐	☐
5. Nina doesn't exercise regularly.	☐	☐	☐
6. Nina doesn't eat healthy foods.	☐	☐	☐

18 **Are you in shape? Do you have a healthy diet? Explain your answers.**

I don't have a healthy diet. I almost never eat vegetables . . .

19 **Read the articles on page 70 of the Student's Book again. Answer the questions.**

Extra reading comprehension

1. Why can't Mark Zupan move his arms and legs normally? _____

2. What is Zupan's nickname? _____

3. What sport does he play? _____

4. What does he do to stay in shape? _____

5. What does he do in his free time? _____

6. What is Bethany Hamilton's sport? _____

7. How did Hamilton lose her arm? _____

8. What does she do when she's not surfing? _____

9. What is her advice? _____

A **Rewrite each sentence. Use <u>can</u> or <u>can't</u>.**

1. Eric is going surfing this weekend.

   Eric can go surfing this weekend. _____

2. Tana and Glenn aren't playing golf on Sunday.

   _____

3. Are we sleeping late tomorrow?

   _____

4. My stepsister isn't going to the movies with us.

   _____

B **Rewrite each sentence. Use <u>have to</u> or <u>don't have to</u>.**

1. We're cleaning the house on Saturday.

   We have to clean the house on Saturday. _____

2. Are the salespeople working late tonight?

   _____

3. Kelly and Caroline are studying for the test tomorrow.

   _____

4. We're not buying a new printer.

   _____

C **Look at the responses. Write information questions with <u>can</u>.**

1. **A:** *Where can I go running* _____?
   B: Well, you can run in the park.

2. **A:** _____?
   B: I think she can come after class, but I'm not sure.

3. **A:** _____?
   B: Three. I speak Spanish, English, and Japanese.

4. **A:** _____?
   B: I can meet you at 9:30.

5. **A:** _____?
   B: Not very often. Golf is so expensive around here.

D Look at the responses. Write information questions with <u>have to</u>.

1. **A:** <u>How often do you have to</u> _____ see your doctor?
   B: Not very often. Just once a year.

2. **A:** _____ meet the client tomorrow?
   B: I have to meet him at the airport.

3. **A:** _____ pick up the car?
   B: You have to pick it up before 5:00. They close early today.

4. **A:** _____ work late tonight?
   B: Because she has a big meeting tomorrow.

5. **A:** _____ get at the supermarket?
   B: We need to get some chicken and broccoli for dinner tonight.

E Complete the sentences. Circle the letter.

1. I _____ about lunch. What do you want?
   a. think   **b.** am thinking   **c.** thinks

2. He _____ her very much now.
   a. love   **b.** is loving   **c.** loves

3. Michelle can't come to the phone. She _____.
   a. sleep   **b.** sleeping   **c.** is sleeping

4. They _____ the chef at that restaurant.
   a. are knowing   **b.** know   **c.** am knowing

5. We _____ some soup for dinner. Would you like some?
   a. am having   **b.** has   **c.** are having

F Unscramble the words to write sentences in the simple present tense.

1. she / a lot / swimming / not / go
   <u>She doesn't go swimming a lot.</u>

2. walk / Joel / to school / sometimes
   _____

3. always / my sisters / on the weekend / me / call
   _____

4. every day / meet / not / their / class
   _____

5. cook dinner / not / usually / on Friday nights / I
   _____

6. they / three times a week / play tennis / generally
   _____

A Correct the capitalization and punctuation in the sentences.

1. I'm crazy about basketball, soccer, and golf.

2. my stepbrother burns more than 3000 calories a day

3. sometimes i have a candy bar for lunch

4. how often do you exercise

5. max hates to play sports but he loves to watch sports on tv

6. what do you generally eat for breakfast

7. they have to clean the house go shopping and study on weekends

8. is there a park a track or an athletic field near your home

9. rose avoids red meat junk food soda and sweets

10. how many hours do you usually sleep

B Choose two questions from Exercise A. Rewrite the questions with correct capitalization and punctuation and write your own answers. Explain your answers.

Q:	
A:	
Q:	
A:	

1 **Match the activities for Dublin, Ireland, with the types of interests. Write the letter on the line.**

_____ 1. play golf on an island in Dublin Bay

_____ 2. enjoy fresh, local seafood

_____ 3. see the 1,200-year-old Book of Kells at Trinity College

_____ 4. visit the Dublin Zoo in Phoenix Park

_____ 5. watch a performance of traditional Irish music and song

a. history

b. entertainment

c. physical activities

d. good food

e. family activities

2 **What do you like to do on vacation? Number the boxes in order, making number 1 your favorite.**

_____ take pictures

_____ go shopping

_____ eat in restaurants

_____ visit museums

_____ swim

_____ lie in the sun

_____ watch movies or shows

_____ go windsurfing

_____ go snorkeling

_____ walk around and explore

_____ go fishing

_____ play golf

3 **In your country, where would you go on vacation for . . .**

good food and entertainment?	**history and culture?**
family activities?	**physical activities?**

4 Complete the conversations. Write the best response on the lines. Use sentences from the box.

I'm fine, thanks.	That's too bad.	It was pretty long and boring.
Well, that's good.	Not too bad, actually.	

5 Write statements. Use the words in parentheses and <u>was</u>, <u>were</u>, <u>wasn't</u>, or <u>weren't</u>.

1. (The cruise / terrific) *The cruise was terrific.* _____

2. (The shops / quite nice) _____

3. (Our room / really small) _____

4. (There / not / many family activities) _____

5. (There / a lot of friendly people) _____

6. (The flight / not / very long) _____

6 Write <u>yes</u> / <u>no</u> questions and short answers. Use the past tense of <u>be</u>.

1. **A:** (your / bus trip / long) *Was your bus trip long* _____?
   B: No, *it wasn't*. It was less than an hour.

2. **A:** (the movie theater / open) _____?
   B: Yes, _____. They had a late show.

3. **A:** (the weather / good) _____?
   B: No, _____. It rained every day.

4. **A:** (there / a movie / on your flight) _____?
   B: No, _____. It was so boring!

5. **A:** (there / many people / on the train) _____?
   B: Yes, _____. We had to stand.

7 Complete the conversation with information questions. Use the past tense of <u>be</u>.

A: Hey, Marty. _____?
   1. Where / you / last weekend
B: My wife and I took a little vacation.

A: Really? _____?
   2. How / it
B: Too short! But we stayed at a great resort.

A: Oh yeah? _____?
   3. Where / the resort
B: Over in Wroxton. We drove up Friday night.

A: Wroxton? That's rather far. _____?
   4. How long / the drive
B: About three and a half hours. There wasn't any traffic.

A: Nice! _____?
   5. And / how / the weather
B: Actually, the weather was quite good. Only rained once!

A: Sounds wonderful. _____?
   6. How long / you / there
B: Just three days. We didn't want to come home!

8 Answer the questions. Use your own words.

1. "When was your last trip?" (YOU) _____

2. "How was the trip?" (YOU) _____

3. "How was the weather?" (YOU) _____

9 **Complete the chart with the present or simple past tense.**

	Present tense	Simple past tense
1.	call	
2.		arrived
3.		studied
4.	get	
5.	stop	

	Present tense	Simple past tense
6.		went
7.	buy	
8.	do	
9.	leave	
10.		ate

10 **Complete the sentences with the simple past tense.**

1. I _____ some nice souvenirs, but I _____
   buy   not spend
   a lot of money.

2. We _____ to Montreal, but we _____
   fly   take
   the train back.

3. We _____ a great time at the baseball game!
   have
   The kids _____ hot dogs and _____ soda,
   eat   drink
   and they _____ the game, too—a little!
   watch

4. I _____ on Friday night. I _____ back at
   leave   get
   noon on Sunday.

11 **Read the responses. Write questions in the simple past tense, using the words in parentheses. Use question words when necessary.**

1. **A:** (you / eat) _Where did you eat_ _____?
   B: We ate at a Japanese restaurant.

2. **A:** (you / go with) _____?
   B: I went with Janine.

3. **A:** (you / like / the art exhibit) _____?
   B: No, I didn't. It was kind of boring.

4. **A:** (you / leave) _____?
   B: We left on Tuesday morning.

5. **A:** (she / buy) _____?
   B: She bought some T-shirts.

6. **A:** (he / play tennis) _____?
   B: He played at the courts at his hotel.

7. **A:** (you / stay) _____?
   B: We stayed a little over a month.

12 Choose the correct responses to complete the conversation. Write the letter on the line.

A: Hi, Emily. I didn't see you at the gym last week.

B: _____
1.

A: Really? Where did you go?

B: _____
2.

A: No kidding! How was it?

B: _____
3.

A: That sounds incredible. Did you and your husband get to go out?

B: _____
4.

a. We visited my sister in California and took the kids to Disneyland.

b. Yes, we did. My sister baby-sat, and we ate at some really nice restaurants.

c. I didn't go. We were on vacation.

d. Fantastic. The kids had so much fun.

13 Answer the questions. Use your own words.

1. "Where did you go on your last vacation?"

YOU _____

2. "Did you have a good time?"

YOU _____

3. "What did you do?"

YOU _____

LESSONS 3 and 4

14 Read the vacation ads on page 80 of the Student's Book again. Circle T for <u>true</u> or F for <u>false</u> about each statement. Find words in the text to support your answers.

Extra reading comprehension

(T) F 1. The Chilean vacation was scenic.
. . . the views of the Andes Mountains were amazing!

T F 2. The Thai vacation was expensive.
_____

T F 3. The Tajikistan vacation was short.
_____

T F 4. The Watanabes wished their Thai vacation were longer.
_____

T F 5. There wasn't time for shopping on Mr. Reyes's trip.
_____

T F 6. Ms. Nack enjoyed good food in Chile.
_____

Look at the vacation picture.

Now read the statements. Who is speaking? Match each statement to a person in the picture. Write the letter on the line.

We ate at the hotel restaurant. The food was awful.

1. _____

The entertainment was terrible. They only had one musician— and he needed guitar lessons!

4. _____

Someone stole my bag! I lost all of my money and my passport.

2. _____

The local beverages were terrific. I had a drink made of coconut milk every day at the beach.

5. _____

I went parasailing. A boat pulled me up high in the air. It was really exciting!

3. _____

16 Complete the vacation postcard. Use adjectives from the box.

scary	relaxing	perfect	terrible	scenic	unusual

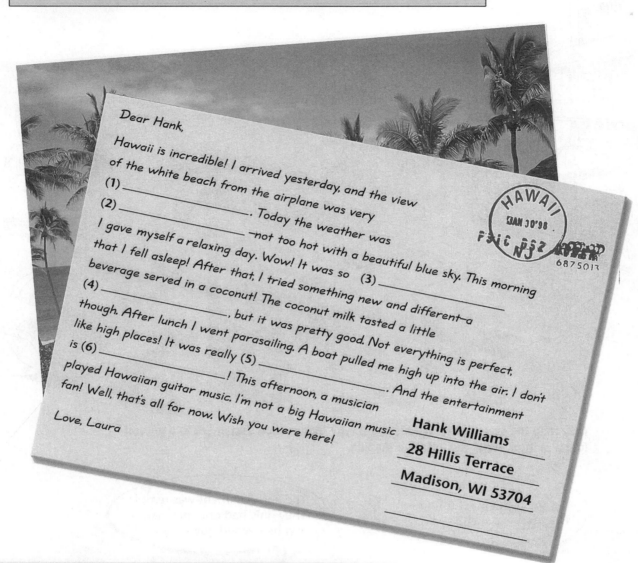

Dear Hank,

Hawaii is incredible! I arrived yesterday, and the view of the white beach from the airplane was very (1) _____. Today the weather was (2) _____—not too hot with a beautiful blue sky. This morning I gave myself a relaxing day. Wow! It was so (3) _____ that I fell asleep! After that, I tried something new and different—a beverage served in a coconut! The coconut milk tasted a little (4) _____, but it was pretty good. Not everything is perfect, though. After lunch I went parasailing. A boat pulled me high up into the air. I don't like high places! It was really (5) _____. And the entertainment is (6) _____! This afternoon, a musician played Hawaiian guitar music. I'm not a big Hawaiian music fan! Well, that's all for now. Wish you were here!

Love, Laura

Hank Williams

28 Hillis Terrace

Madison, WI 53704

HAWAII
JAN 30'98
PSIC DSZ NJ
6875013

GRAMMAR BOOSTER

A Choose the correct response. Write the letter on the line.

_____ 1. "How was your vacation?"

_____ 2. "Where did you go?"

_____ 3. "How long were you there?"

_____ 4. "Was the weather good?"

_____ 5. "How were the rooms?"

_____ 6. "Were there a lot of things to do?"

_____ 7. "Was the food OK?"

a. No, it wasn't. It rained all week.

b. Terrific. It was so much fun.

c. Jamaica.

d. Yes, there were. We were busy all the time.

e. Yes, it was good. But a little spicy.

f. Just a week.

g. Clean and comfortable.

B Correct the errors in the e-mail message.

Dear Mari,

             was
My vacation ~~were~~ lots of fun! My family and I went to Hawaii. The only problem

were the hotel. It was very nice. The beds were terrible. Everything else were

perfect. There was many activities. My favorite activity wasn't parasailing. It were

terrific.

Laura

C Write questions with the past tense of <u>be</u>. Then answer the questions with complete sentences. Use your own words.

1. when / your last vacation _____?
    YOU _____

2. it / long _____?
    YOU _____

3. the hotel / nice _____?
    YOU _____

4. how / the weather _____?
    YOU _____

5. how many / people / with you _____?
    YOU _____

D Complete the paragraph. Use the simple past tense of words from the box. Some words can be used more than once.

drink	stop	travel	take	shop	watch	be	walk

       In January, I _____ to Morocco with my friend Nan. We explored
           1.

the narrow streets of the medieval medina in Marrakech. The medina is closed to

traffic. So, there _____ no cars, but there _____ a lot of donkeys.
             2.   3.

We _____ for hours and _____ often to look at the beautiful
    4.   5.

carpets for sale. We _____ for inexpensive leather goods, _____
                6.   7.

mint tea, and _____ street performers. We wandered all afternoon. We
            8.

got lost, and then we _____ a taxi back to our hotel.
             9.

E Rewrite the sentences. Use the simple past tense and a past time expression.

1. We go to the beach every year. _We went to the beach last year._

2. The weather isn't very nice today. _____

3. We don't stay in a hotel. _____

4. I often cook clams at the beach. _____

5. Everyone has a good time. _____

6. What do you do in the summer? _____

F Read the statements. Write questions to ask for more information, using the words in parentheses.

1. A: She bought a new printer. B: _Why did she buy a new printer_ ? (why)

2. A: She went on vacation. B: _____? (where)

3. A: They went to the gym. B: _____? (when)

4. A: I visited some friends. B: _____? (who)

5. A: He spent a lot of money. B: _____? (how much)

WRITING BOOSTER

A Read the sentences about Amy's weekend trip to Chicago with her friends.

1. They all flew to Chicago and met at the airport.

2. They checked into their hotel downtown and got dressed to go out.

3. They saw the musical *Jersey Boys*.

4. On Saturday, they went to the spa.

5. They went shopping on Michigan Avenue.

6. They had a delicious steak dinner at a nice restaurant.

7. They listened to pop music at a concert.

8. They went out fishing .

9. They said good-bye and returned home on Sunday.

B On a separate sheet of paper, write a paragraph about Amy's trip. Use time clauses and time-order transition words.

Let me tell you about Amy's trip to Chicago with her friends. First, . . .

The Top 10 Most Visited Tourist Attractions in the World

1. Times Square—New York City (U.S.)
2. National Mall & Memorial Parks—Washington, D.C. (U.S.)
3. Disney World's Magic Kingdom—Orlando, Florida (U.S.)
4. Trafalgar Square—London (U.K.)
5. Disneyland Park—Anaheim, California (U.S.)
6. Niagara Falls—Canada and U.S.
7. Fisherman's Wharf—San Francisco, California (U.S.)
8. Tokyo Disneyland—Tokyo (Japan)
9. Notre de Dame—Paris (France)
10. Disneyland—Paris (France)

SOURCE: adventure.howstuffworks.com

Shopping for Clothes

Preview

---

1 Label each clothing item with the correct department. Use words from the box.
Write the letter on the line.

| a. Sleepwear | c. Athletic Wear | e. Hosiery |
| b. Underwear & Lingerie | d. Outerwear | f. Bags & Accessories |

_____ 1. coats

_____ 2. sunglasses

_____ 3. slippers

_____ 4. golf shirts

_____ 5. slips

_____ 6. leggings

---

2 What's important to these customers when they shop for footwear?
Write <u>price</u>, <u>selection</u>, or <u>service</u> on the line.

I always shop at Dalton's Department Store because the clerks are really helpful. They always help me find the right size and even offer to gift wrap!

I'm a student so I don't have a lot of money. I shop at Shoe Outlet because they always have a big sale. The shoes I'm wearing now were 50% off!

Jake's Footwear is the best! They have more than 200 different kinds of footwear—boots, sandals, running shoes . . . I like to have a lot of choices when I shop.

1. _____

2. _____

3. _____

3 **Label the clothing items in the picture. Use words from the box.**

pumps

running shoes

a sweatshirt

a blazer

a shirt

a windbreaker

pantyhose

a skirt

socks

sweatpants

1. _____

2. _____

3. _____

4. _____

5. _____

6. _____

7. _____

8. _____

9. _____

10. _____

4 **What's your style? Complete the chart with the clothing and shoes you usually wear.**

At home	At work	At school	To go out

5 **Complete the conversations. Use object pronouns from the box. Pronouns can be used more than once.**

me	you	him	her	it	us	them

1. **A:** Are your sisters going to the party?

   B: I hope so. I invited _____ .

2. **A:** This sweatshirt is really old.

   B: That's OK. I wear _____ to exercise.

3. **A:** Did you meet Ms. Jacobs?

   B: Yes, I met _____ this morning.

4. **A:** When can I call you?

   B: Let's see. Call _____ tomorrow. I'll be home all day.

5. **A:** I didn't see you and Emma at the concert.

   B: You didn't see _____? We were right near the stage.

6. **A:** I'll take the sandals.

   B: Great. Would you like me to gift wrap _____ for _____?

7. **A:** These pants are too small.

   B: Give _____ to your brother.

   A: I can't give _____ to _____. He wears a size 36!

Complete the conversations. Use sentences from the box.

| Charge, please. | That's too bad. | Certainly. | The V-neck or the crew neck? |

Could you gift wrap these shirts?

CASH

1. _____
_____

Did you know that . . .

- the first known pictures of footwear are boots in a 15,000-year-old painting in a cave in Spain?
- in the year 200, Marcus Aurelius, Emperor of Rome, said that only he could wear red sandals?
- before the 1860s, pairs of boots didn't have a right and a left? Both boots were the same.

How would you like to pay?

2. _____
_____

I'm sorry. We don't have these pumps in black.

3. _____
_____

I'll take the sweater.

4. _____
_____

LESSON 2

7

Complete the chart with words from the box. Write the comparative form of each adjective in the correct column.

loose	spicy	hot	sweet	comfortable
tall	bad	important	thin	young
friendly	healthy	nice	fat	convenient

1. (+) -r	2. (+) -er	3. (–) -y (+) -ier	4. double the final consonant (+) -er	5. more	6. irregular forms
larger	smaller	heavier	bigger	more expensive	better
					X
X					X

8 **Compare the items in the pictures. Write sentences with comparative adjectives.**
Use words from the box or your own words.

spicy	salty	expensive	portable	young
old	cheap	fast	healthy	large
big	small	comfortable	good	convenient

1.

chili peppers   rice

Chili peppers are spicier than rice.

2.

a desktop   a laptop

_____

3.

a hair dryer   a photocopier

_____

4.

running shoes   pumps

_____

5.

your grandparents   your children

_____

6.

a salad   french fries

_____

7.
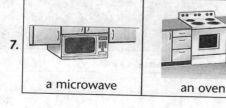
a microwave   an oven

_____

Choose the correct response. Circle the letter.

1. "Do you have this in a medium?"
   a. Thanks.
   b. Here you go.
   c. Yes, please.

2. "How much are these pajamas?"
   a. The Dreams brand ones?
   b. That's not too bad.
   c. These are a large.

3. "Can I try it on?"
   a. Yes, we do.
   b. No, thanks.
   c. Of course!

4. "Thank you for wrapping them for me."
   a. They're $75.
   b. My pleasure.
   c. Yes, please.

10 **Look at the store ad. Then complete the sentences. Use the information in the ad or your own words.**

Big City Footwear

BIG BOOT SALE!

Comfort brand casual boots
Light and very comfortable, perfect for walking!
Available in men's US sizes 7-14.
Light Brown, Dark Blue, Black
US$25.00

A great low price!

Arctic brand winter boots
Your feet will thank you in cold weather!
Waterproof and heavy weight for safety on ice and snow.
Available in men's US sizes 7, 12, 13, 14.
Dark Brown, Black
US$55.00

Warm, Warm, Warm!

Downtown brand dress boots
Knee-high, 3 inch (7.6 cm) heel.
Be fashionable going out or going to work!
Available in women's US sizes 5-10.
Black, Dark Red, Grey, Dark Green
US$90.00

1. The Comfort brand boots are _____ than the Downtown boots.

2. The Big City Footwear store has the Arctic brand boots in brown and _____.

3. The Downtown brand boots are _____ than the Arctic brand boots.

4. The Arctic brand boots are _____ than the Comfort brand boots.

5. The Big City Footwear store has the Downtown brand boots in sizes _____.

11 **Complete the sentences. Use your own ideas and the cues in parentheses.**

1. _____ is more expensive than _____. (two clothing stores)

2. _____ is better than _____. (two restaurants)

3. _____ is more popular than _____. (two music genres)

4. _____ is warmer than _____. (two travel destinations)

5. _____ is more exciting than _____. (two physical activities)

12 Look at the store floor plan. Start at the Information desk. Follow the directions. Where are you? Write the name of the department on the line.

1. That's on this floor. Walk to the back of the store. It's on the left side, just past Hosiery.

   Where are you?

   _____

2. Take the elevator to the second floor. Turn left when you get off. Then turn right at Men's Outerwear. It's between Men's Outerwear and Men's Underwear.

   Where are you?

   _____

3. Go down the escalator to the basement and walk to the front of the store. You'll see it on the right.

   Where are you?

   _____

Second Floor

Elevators
Stairs
Men's Outerwear
Men's Shoes
Men's Athletic Wear
Men's Underwear
Men's Casual
Men's Sleepwear
Rear Entrance

First Floor
Stairs Elevators
Lingerie
Women's Shoes
You are here
Hosiery
Information
Bags/Accessories
Women's Casual
Front Entrance

Stairs Elevators
Electronics
Photo Studio
Small Appliances
Restaurant
Basement

13 Match the descriptions with similar meanings. Write the letter on the line.

_____ 1. informal   a. modest

_____ 2. liberal   b. casual

_____ 3. conservative   c. showing too much skin

_____ 4. revealing   d. "anything goes"

14

Extra reading comprehension

Read the travel blog on page 94 of the Student's Book again. What clothing is appropriate for women traveling in Tanzania? Complete the chart of do's and don'ts.

Do's	Don'ts

15 Choose one of the travel destinations below. What clothing will you pack for the trip? Make a list. Include any shoes, outerwear, casual, formal, conservative, or wild clothes you will need.

Go skiing in the Swiss Alps.	Hear gospel music at a Harlem church in New York City, USA.	Go exercise at a club in Paris, France.	Go swimming on Boracay Island, Philippines.

GRAMMAR BOOSTER

A Write questions to ask for more information. Use object pronouns and the words in parentheses.

1. A: I take my grandmother to the same restaurant every week.
   B: _Where do you take her_ ? (where)

2. A: She washes her car a lot.
   B: _____? (when)

3. A: He eats sandwiches for lunch.
   B: _____? (how often)

4. A: Monica meets her friend for coffee every day.
   B: _____? (what time)

B Write sentences in two ways, using the words indicated. Add prepositions if necessary.

1. the address / give / her
   Give her the address.
   Give the address to her.

2. Tina / gifts / him / buys
   _____
   _____

3. the teacher / homework / us / gave
   _____
   _____

4. the waiters / them / their lunch / served
   _____
   _____

5. Ann / a shirt / her son / bought
   _____
   _____

6. the clerk / me / a smaller size / found
   _____
   _____

C Complete the sentences with words from the box. Use the comparative form.

relaxing	healthy	comfortable	nice	warm	fast	big

1. A turtleneck is _____ than a V-neck.

2. Flats are _____ than pumps.

3. Athletic fields are usually _____ than tennis courts.

4. Salads are _____ than fries.

5. The expensive suit isn't _____ than the inexpensive one. It's just more expensive.

6. I don't like to fly, but it's _____ than taking the train.

7. A spa vacation is _____ than a business trip.

D Answer the questions in complete sentences. Use your own words.

1. "Which is easier—speaking or writing in English?"

YOU _____

2. "Where are you happier—at home or on vacation?"

YOU _____

3. "Which is more interesting—shopping for clothes or shopping for electronics?"

YOU _____

WRITING BOOSTER

A Check the sentence with the clearer meaning.

1. ☐ We're going to a restaurant since we don't have any food at home.
   ☐ We don't have any food at home since we're going to a restaurant.

2. ☐ We're going to the beach because I packed my swimsuit.
   ☐ I packed my swimsuit because we're going to the beach.

3. ☐ Because we're shopping for a new one, our computer is obsolete.
   ☐ Because our computer is obsolete, we're shopping for a new one.

4. ☐ Since he didn't have cash, he used his credit card.
   ☐ Since he used his credit card, he didn't have cash.

B Answer each of the following questions with a complete sentence containing a clause with <u>because</u> or <u>since</u>. Use your own words.

Example: Do you like shopping for clothes online?
I don't like shopping for clothes online because I can't try them on.

1. "Do you like going to concerts?"

YOU _____

2. "Which is better—a large family or a small family?"

YOU _____

3. "Do you like eating at home or eating in a restaurant?"

YOU _____

4. "When you go on vacation, do you like going to big cities or small towns?"

YOU _____

Taking Transportation

1 Look at the departure schedule and the clock.
Read the statements. Check <u>true</u> or <u>false</u>.

RAPID AIR BRASILIA DEPARTURES

Destination	FLT/No.	Departs	Gate	Status
São Paulo	56	15:50	G4	departed
Belo Horizonte	267	16:10	G3	boarding
Rio de Janeiro	89	16:10	G9	boarding
São Paulo	58	16:50	G4	now 17:25
São Luis	902	17:00	G3	on time
São Paulo	60	17:50	G4	delayed
Porto Alegre	763	17:50	G3	on time
Caracas	04	18:05	G1	canceled
Rio de Janeiro	91	18:10	G9	on time
São Paulo	62	18:50	G4	on time

15:50

	true	false
1. The next flight to Porto Alegre is at 5:50 P.M.	☐	☐
2. Flight 902 to São Luis is leaving from Gate G4.	☐	☐
3. The flight to Caracas is delayed.	☐	☐
4. Flight number 267 is going to Belo Horizonte.	☐	☐
5. Passengers traveling to Rio de Janeiro on Flight 89 should hurry.	☐	☐
6. Flight 60 to São Paulo is late.	☐	☐

2 Choose the correct response. Write the letter on the line.

_____ 1. "Oh, no! The bus is leaving in four minutes."

_____ 2. "Good news. Our flight is on time."

_____ 3. "I'm looking for Gate C4."

_____ 4. "Is this your final destination?"

_____ 5. "I'm on my way to Barcelona, too."

_____ 6. "We're catching the 8:27 train, right?"

a. Thank goodness.

b. No, I'm connecting to Quito.

c. What a coincidence!

d. Yes. Let's look for track 6.

e. It's down this hall, on the right.

f. We should hurry!

LESSON 1

3 Answer the questions in complete sentences.

1. Which is faster—the local or the express?

_____

2. Which is more scenic—an aisle seat or a window seat?

_____

3. Which is more convenient—a direct flight or a non-stop flight?

_____

4. Which is less expensive—a one-way ticket or a round-trip ticket?

_____

4 **Complete each sentence or question. Use <u>could</u> or <u>should</u> and the base form of the verb.**

1. Want my advice? _____ the express. _____ the local, but it takes
   You / take   You / take
   thirty minutes longer.

2. _____! _____ the 7:30!
   You / hurry   You / make

3. _____ round-trip tickets. They are cheaper than two one-way tickets, and she won't
   She / buy
   have to wait in another ticket line.

4. _____ an aisle seat in the rear of the plane or a window seat in the front. What do
   We / take
   you think? Which seats _____?
   we / take

5. The flight is delayed. _____ late for the meeting. _____ the office?
   We / be   we / call

6. No, _____ a direct flight. They have to change planes in Anchorage.
   they / not / get

5 **Put the conversation in order. Write the number on the line.**

_____ Let's see. The local leaves from track 23, lower level.

_1_ Can I help you?

_____ Oh, no! What should we do?

_____ That's not too bad. What's the track number?

_____ Yes. Can we still make the 10:05 express to Antwerp?

_____ I'm sorry. You missed it.

_____ Thanks very much.

_____ Well, you could take a local train. There's one at 11:05.

6 **Look at the schedules. Which train should the people take?**
Write your advice on the line.

Metropolitan Railroad			
	Local	**Express**	**Local**
White Plains	7:25	8:22	9:05
Scarsdale	7:42	-	9:22
Bronxville	8:05	-	9:40
Harlem 125th St.	8:24	-	9:59
Grand Central—New York City	8:30	8:59	10:06

I live in White Plains. I need a train that will arrive in New York City around 9:00 A.M. Could I take the 8:22 express?

1. _Yes, you could_
   take the 8:22.

I live in White Plains. I'm meeting my boss at Grand Central Station at 8:45 A.M., and I can't be late. Which train should I take?

2. _____
   _____

I live in Scarsdale. I need to shop for a new laptop in New York City. Most computer stores open at 10:00 A.M. What time should I be at the Scarsdale train station?

3. _____
   _____

I'm in White Plains. I want to go to Bronxville. Could I take an express train or should I take a local?

4. _____
   _____

7 **What are your plans for today? Check the things you're going to do. Add your own activities.**

- ☐ call a friend
- ☐ check my e-mail
- ☐ go shopping
- ☐ study
- ☐ exercise
- ☐ clean my house
- ☐ take the bus
- ☐ cook
- ☐ other _____

8 **Now write sentences about your plans for today. Use the future tense with <u>be going to</u>.**

I'm going to call a friend tonight after work.

9 **What are they going to do? Write the letter on the line.**

_____ **1.** She's going to make a reservation.

_____ **2.** He's going to arrive at 8:45.

_____ **3.** She's going to take a limo.

_____ **4.** He's not going to take a taxi.

10 Read the response. Complete each question with <u>be going to</u>.

1. A: Where *is Paul going to meet us* _____?
   B: Paul's going to meet us at the airport café.

2. A: Who _____?
   B: I think Gretchen is going to buy the tickets.

3. A: When _____?
   B: I'm going to pack tonight.

4. A: What time _____?
   B: They're going to arrive at 5:50 P.M.

5. A: _____ our connecting flight?
   B: Yes, we'll make it.

> The world's longest direct run train (without changing trains) is 10,214 km, from Moscow, Russia, to Pyongyang, North Korea. One train a week takes this route. The trip takes almost eight days!
>
> **SOURCE:** www.guinnessworldrecords.com

11 Complete the conversation. Use words from the box.

limousine	going	should	late	check	arriving	reservation	rental

A: What time are we _____ in Copenhagen?
1.

B: Pretty _____. Around 10:30 P.M.
2.

A: What about a hotel?

B: I'm going to make a _____ online.
3.

A: Great. And are we _____ to need a taxi to the hotel?
4.

B: There's a _____ from the airport, or we could
5.
get a _____ car.
6.

A: They're expensive. We _____ save our money.
7.
Is there a train?

B: Let me _____ . . .
8.

LESSONS 3 and 4

12 Complete the conversation. Use words from the box.

gate	make	check	land	delayed	depart
go through security		departure lounge		boarding passes	

1. **Passenger A:** Do we need to check in?

   Passenger B: No, we don't. I printed our _____ online and we're not
   1.
   checking any luggage.

   Passenger A: OK. Let's check a monitor for our _____ number and then
   2.
   we should _____.
   3.

2. Passenger: Excuse me. Is Flight 68 going to _____ on time?
4.
   Agent: No, I'm sorry. The flight is _____. Have a seat in the _____.
5.   6.
   We'll make an announcement when we're ready for boarding.

3. Passenger: Excuse me. What time are we going to _____?
7.
   Flight Attendant: Let me _____ . . . Our new arrival time is 8:23.
8.
   Passenger: 8:23? My connecting flight is at 8:40. Can I still _____ it?
9.

13 **Read the article.**

Summary Air Travel Tips

Traveling by air in the summer can be frustrating. There are delayed flights, late arrivals, and missed connections. Flights are full and crowded since airlines overbook them. If you can, avoid air travel during this peak season and plan your vacation for a less busy time of the year. If you have to fly during the summer, here are some ideas to make it a little easier:

- Don't fly after 2:00 P.M. There are often summer thunderstorms in the late afternoon. They could cause flights to be delayed or canceled.

- Fly early in the morning. Later flights are often affected by delayed flights earlier in the day.

- Fly on Tuesday, Wednesday, Thursday, or Saturday. Sunday, Monday, and Friday are the busiest air-travel days.

- Check airport security do's and don'ts online before you arrive at the airport.

- Take food and water on board in case of a long delay before takeoff. Remember to purchase food and beverages after you go through airport security.

- Expect delays. If you're arriving at 7:00 P.M., don't make a dinner reservation for 7:30.

Source: christinecolumbus.com

Now give advice based on the article. Underline the best option. Then write a sentence with <u>should</u>.

Which is better . . .

1. taking a vacation in summer or <u>in spring</u>?

   You should take a vacation in spring.

2. booking a 9:00 A.M. flight or a 3:00 P.M. flight?

   _____

3. traveling on a Monday or a Tuesday?

   _____

4. checking airport security regulations at home or at the airport?

   _____

5. bringing food and drinks from home, buying them at the airport, or getting them on the plane?

   _____

6. planning to arrive on time or planning to arrive late?

   _____

14 Look at the pictures of Joe Kelly's trip. Then read the statements. Check <u>true</u> or <u>false</u>.

	true	false
1. His flight was on time.	☐	☐
2. He sat in an aisle seat.	☐	☐
3. His plane had mechanical problems.	☐	☐
4. He missed the hotel shuttle bus.	☐	☐
5. He drove a rental car to the hotel.	☐	☐

15 Write a short paragraph about Joe Kelly's trip.

16

Extra reading comprehension

Read the article "Get bumped from a flight?" on page 106 of the Student's Book again. Match words and phrases from the article with their meanings.

_____ 1. overbook

_____ 2. "no-shows"

_____ 3. get bumped

_____ 4. volunteer

_____ 5. perks

_____ 6. deplane

a. have to get off the plane because there aren't enough seats

b. someone who offers to get off an overbooked flight

c. get off the plane

d. sell too many tickets for a flight

e. benefits like cash, free flights, hotels, and meals

f. people who have tickets but don't appear for a flight

17

Extra reading comprehension

Read the articles on page 106 of the Student's Book again. Answer the questions.

1. Why do airlines overbook flights?

_____

2. What do airlines give bumped passengers?

_____

3. Why did Mr. Carter turn onto the train tracks?

_____

4. Were Mr. Carter and his son in the car when the train hit it?

_____

5. What advice do the police officers give?

_____

GRAMMAR BOOSTER

A **Read the questions and statements. Correct the mistakes.**

1. You should ~~to go~~ *go to* track 57.

2. Where could he to get a train to Paris?

3. Rebecca can't takes a flight to Tokyo.

4. When we should leave?

5. How late can he to board?

6. He shoulds choose an aisle seat.

B **Read the questions. Complete the responses.**

1. A: Should she take the local?

   B: No, _she shouldn't_. It's too slow.

2. A: Can he bring food on the flight?

   B: Yes, _____.

3. A: Could I take the number 3 train?

   B: Yes, _____. It will take you to the right station.

4. A: Can we get seats together?

   B: No, _____. I'm sorry. We only have a few seats left.

5. A: Should they get a rental car?

   B: Yes, _____. It's more convenient.

C Rewrite the sentences. Use a different way to express future actions. There may be more than one correct answer.

1. I'm studying all day tomorrow.

   _____

2. I'm going to run three miles on Saturday.

   _____

3. The train departs in twenty minutes.

   _____

4. The test is going to be next week.

   _____

5. The ship is going to arrive in Halifax tomorrow morning.

   _____

WRITING BOOSTER

A Think about two vacation destinations you know of and could recommend to others. Complete the chart.

	Destination 1	Destination 2
Where?		
What kind of transportation?		
What time of year?		
What to see / do?		
What to bring?		
Where / What to eat?		
How long to stay?		

B On a separate sheet of paper, write two paragraphs about the vacation destinations you recommend. Give advice and suggest alternatives or possibilities. Use <u>should</u> and <u>could</u>. Start the first paragraph like this.

I recommend _____ as your next vacation destination. . . .

Start the second paragraph like this:

Another good destination for your next vacation is _____ . . .

UNIT 10

Preview

Shopping Smart

a. Take your ATM card.

b. Enter the amount of cash you want.

c. Take your cash.

d. Put your ATM card in the card slot.

e. Choose your language.

f. Enter your Personal Identification Number (PIN).

1 How do you use an ATM machine? Look at the pictures below. Match each picture with an instruction from the box.

1. ____

2. ____

◄ ENGLISH
◄ SPANISH

3. ____

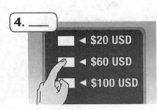
4. ____

◄ $20 USD
◄ $60 USD
◄ $100 USD

5. ____

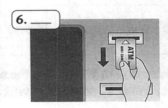
6. ____

2 Match the financial terms with their definitions. Write the letter on the line.

____ 1. an ATM

____ 2. cash

____ 3. foreign currency

____ 4. a currency exchange

____ 5. an exchange rate

____ 6. a fee

a. money from another country

b. the value of one currency compared to another

c. a machine that you use to get money from your bank account

d. extra charges

e. money in the form of bills or coins (not checks, credit cards, etc.)

f. buying or selling money from another country

3 Answer the questions. Use your own words.

1. "What shop in your city has really nice stuff?"

   YOU _____

2. "Are things in this shop usually affordable or more than you want to spend?"

   YOU _____

3. "Is it OK to bargain for a lower price in this shop?"

   YOU _____

4. "In your city, where is it OK to bargain?"

   YOU _____

5. "Are you good at bargaining?"

   YOU _____

4 Look at the chart from a digital camera buying guide.

COMPARE DIGITAL CAMERAS					KEY	
Brand / Model	Price	Ease of Use	Size	Weight	••••	very easy
Diego Mini 3000	US$239	••	c	35 g (1.2 oz)	•••	pretty easy
Honshu B100	US$209	•••	p	283 g (9.9 oz)	••	a little difficult
Honshu X24	US$139	•	s	180 g (6.3 oz)	•	difficult
Prego 5	US$299	••••	s	135 g (4.7 oz)	c	compact (small size, can fit in a shirt pocket)
Vision 2.0	US$449	•••	s	224 g (7.9 oz)	s	standard (medium size, similar to a point and shoot camera)
					p	professional (large size, similar to a 35mm camera)

Now write questions with <u>Which</u>. Use the superlative form of the adjectives from the box.
For some items, it may be possible to write more than one question.

expensive	light	portable	easy to use	cheap	heavy	difficult to use

1. A: _Which camera is the most expensive_ _____?
   B: The Vision 2.0.

2. A: _____?
   B: The Honshu X24.

3. A: _____?
   B: The Diego Mini 3000.

4. A: _____?
   B: The Prego 5.

5. A: _____?
   B: The Honshu B100.

5 Read each person's statement. For each shopper, recommend a digital camera
from the buying guide in Exercise 4. Give a reason for your advice.

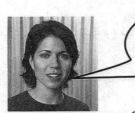

"I need a new camera. The
one I have now is too heavy.
I really want a camera that I can
carry in my jacket pocket."

1. **YOU** _____

"I'm looking for a digital camera for my mother. She isn't good with electronics, so it must be very easy to use. What do you recommend?"

2. YOU _____

"I'd like to have a look at your least expensive digital camera. I can't spend more that $150. Do you have anything in my price range?"

3. YOU _____

6 **Choose the correct response. Circle the letter.**

1. "This camera isn't in my price range."
   a. How much can you spend?
   b. Would you like to take it?
   c. Can I have a look?

2. "Why is this smart phone the best?"
   a. It's the heaviest.
   b. It's the fastest.
   c. It's the most difficult to use.

3. "I can't spend more than $200."
   a. Have a look at our best model.
   b. How would you like to pay for it?
   c. Let me show you something in your price range.

4. "Can I have a look?"
   a. Certainly.
   b. Really?
   c. Excuse me.

7 **Complete the conversation. Write the letter on the line.**

A: Can I help you?

B: _____
      1.

A: OK. Which one are you interested in?

B: _____
      2.

A: The Muze HD. It's the most popular.

B: _____
      3.

A: What about the XTunes? It's pretty good, and it's more affordable.

B: _____
      4.

A: No. And the sound is great.

B: _____
      5.

A: And how would you like to pay for it?

B: _____
      6.

a. Actually, that's a little out of my price range.

b. Cash, please.

c. Yes, please. I'm looking for an MP3 player for my son.

d. Is it difficult to use?

e. OK. I'll take the XTunes.

f. I don't know. What do you recommend?

8 Complete the sentences. Use <u>too</u> or <u>enough</u> and the adjective.

1. I'm not going to read that book. It's _____.
   boring
2. Sirena shouldn't travel alone. She isn't _____.
   old
3. I don't want to buy anything in that shop. The people were _____.
   unfriendly
4. Talia likes the red rug, but it's _____ for her living room.
   big
5. I love this belt, but it isn't _____. I need a bigger size.
   long
6. Are your shoes _____? We're going to do a lot of walking.
   comfortable
7. We wanted to bargain for a lower price, but it was _____.
   difficult

9 Complete the conversations. Use words from the box.

too	deal	much	all	low
more	have	bowl	enough	give

A: This _____ is gorgeous. I'd love to get it for my sister.
          1.
B: It's nice. And it's small _____ to take in your suitcase.
                              2.
A: I'm going to ask about the price. I hope it's not _____ expensive.
                                                      3.

• • •

A: I'm interested in this bowl. How _____ do you want for it?
                                    4.
C: This one is $60.

A: That's _____ than I want to spend.
          5.
C: I could go as _____ as $50.
                  6.
A: I can _____ you $30 for it.
         7.
C: You can _____ it for $40. That's a bargain.
            8.
A: _____ I have is $35.
   9.
C: OK. It's a _____.
              10.

10 Choose the correct response. Write the letter on the line.

_____ 1. "$650! I paid $429 for the same camcorder yesterday!"

_____ 2. "How much did you pay for that vase?"

_____ 3. "Should I try to get a better price?"

_____ 4. "I saved a lot of money on this DVD player. It was only $79."

_____ 5. "Here you are, sir. The Atlas Hotel. That's $8.50."

a. It can't hurt to ask.

b. What a total rip-off!

c. Thanks. Keep the change.

d. What a great deal!

e. Only $20. It was a real bargain.

11 Read the article about bargaining customs around the world.
Then read the statements. Check <u>true</u> or <u>false</u>.

Can you give me a better price?

Bargaining Customs around the World

Bargaining customs are very different around the world. Few would go shopping in another country without knowing the exchange rate. However, many travelers don't learn anything about the local shopping customs of the place they are visiting before spending money. Understanding when it's OK to bargain can save you a lot of money and make your shopping experience much more enjoyable.

In some countries, bargaining is an important part of the shopping culture. In others, bargaining is not done at all. Here's a bargaining guide for some countries around the world:

Morocco: Bargaining is always expected in the shopping markets. Here bargaining is more than just getting the best price. If you go into a shop and agree to the first price a seller offers, the seller may not be happy. For Moroccans, bargaining is a form of entertainment; it's a game of skill, a little bit of acting, and it's a chance to chat about the weather, business, and family. So be sure to have fun and try to get a better price!

Switzerland: Bargaining is not the custom here. Shop clerks can almost never give you a lower price. However, some hotels may give you a lower rate during the less popular times of year. It can't hurt to ask.

Tahiti: Bargaining is not appropriate in the South Pacific. In fact, it is considered disrespectful to ask for a better price. In the food markets, sellers will even take their fruits and vegetables back home with them, rather than give a discount!

SOURCE: "Lonely Planet Travel Guides"

	true	false
1. Bargaining customs are similar around the world.	☐	☐
2. Generally, market sellers in Morocco love to bargain.	☐	☐
3. In Switzerland, it's OK to bargain for a cheaper hotel room.	☐	☐
4. It can't hurt to ask a fruit seller in Tahiti for a lower price.	☐	☐

12 Read the article on page 116 of the Student's Book again. Then check <u>true</u> or <u>false</u>, according to the article.

Extra reading comprehension

	true	false
1. Tipping is expected in all countries.	☐	☐
2. In U.S. restaurants, a 10% tip is usually enough.	☐	☐
3. In some European countries, you should hand the tip to the waiter.	☐	☐
4. In Germany, you should leave the tip on the table.	☐	☐
5. For a taxi fare of 9.50 pesos in Buenos Aires, give the driver 10 pesos.	☐	☐
6. Australian porters expect a bigger tip than porters in other countries.	☐	☐
7. Tip Japanese porters about US$1 per bag.	☐	☐
8. Tipping isn't customary in Korea.	☐	☐

13 Write a short paragraph about bargaining in your own country. What items do people bargain for? What items do people never bargain for?

GRAMMAR BOOSTER

A Complete the chart.

	Adjective	Comparative form	Superlative form
1.	beautiful		
2.			the most intelligent
3.	big		
4.		more convenient	
5.	busy		
6.			the fastest
7.		safer	
8.	noisy		

B Complete the conversations with the comparative or the superlative form of the adjective in parentheses.

1. **A:** Which one of these three sweaters do you think is _____*the prettiest*_____ (pretty)?

   B: The blue one. The other two are not attractive at all.

2. **A:** How do you like the book?

   B: I don't like it. It's _____ (bad) than the one we read last month.

3. **A:** Did you enjoy Australia?

   B: Yes. I think it's one of _____ (interesting) places in the world.

4. **A:** Who is _____ (good) at baseball, you or your brother?

   B: Well, I'm a _____ (fast) base runner, but my brother is a _____ (powerful) hitter. Actually, my dad is the _____ (good) player in the family. He was a star player in college.

5. **A:** Which one of the two laptops is _____ (popular)?

   B: Well, the X102 is the _____ (cheap) model in the store. But I actually recommend the X200. It's a little _____ (expensive) than the X102, but much _____ (light).

C Answer the questions. Use <u>too</u> or <u>enough</u> and the adjective in parentheses.

1. **A:** Why didn't you buy the camcorder?

   B: (expensive) _____. I need to save money this month.

2. **A:** Is the food too spicy?

   B: (spicy) _____. I'm going to ask for more hot sauce!

3. **A:** What's wrong with these shoes?

   B: I can't wear them. (uncomfortable) _____.

4. **A:** Why don't you like the apartment?

   B: (noisy) _____. I'm looking for a quiet neighborhood.

5. **A:** Why don't you take the train instead of flying?

   B: (fast) _____. I have to get there as soon as possible.

6. **A:** Do you want to go to a pop concert?

   B: Thanks for asking, but I'm not a pop music fan. (boring) _____.

WRITING BOOSTER

A Rewrite each pair of sentences, using the words in parentheses.

1. This rug is a good deal. It's a bit more than I want to spend. (However)
   This rug is a good deal. However, it's a bit more than I want to spend. _____

2. The Trekker jacket is very warm. It's the lightest one. (even though)
   _____

3. Our new coffeemaker is not the most expensive. It makes the best coffee. (However)
   _____

4. Half Moon Café has the best food in town. It's very expensive. (On the other hand)
   _____

5. This is last year's model. The clerk won't give me a lower price. (Even though)
   _____

B Write sentences about the advantages and disadvantages of credit cards and cash. Use the chart in Exercise E on page 111 of the Student's Book. Use <u>Even though</u>, <u>However</u>, and <u>On the other hand</u>.

1. Credit cards: _____
   _____

2. Cash: _____
   _____

C Choose three topics from the list. For each topic, compare their advantages and disadvantages. Use <u>Even though</u>, <u>However</u>, and <u>On the other hand</u>.

> listening to music at home / going to a concert
>
> large family / small family
>
> smart phones / regular cell phones
>
> conservative clothes / wild clothes
>
> air travel / train travel

Listening to music at home is more relaxing. On the other hand, going to a concert is more exciting.

What continent is home to the world's biggest shopping malls?

It's not North America. Only one of the world's ten largest malls is in the U.S. Built in 1969, the Eastwood Mall Complex in Youngstown, Ohio, is the ninth largest mall. Similarly, one Canadian mall made the top-ten list. The West Edmonton Mall in Alberta, built in 1981, is number six.

Europe's biggest mall—fifth on the list of the world's largest—is newer. It was built in 2005. It's located in Istanbul, Turkey.

The continent with the biggest, newest, and most exciting malls is Asia. Seven of the world's ten largest shopping malls are in Asia. The two largest are in China and opened in 2005 and 2004. The New South China Mall in Dongguan has 1500 stores and 7.1 million square feet of retail space. The Golden Resources Mall in Beijing—also called "The Great Mall of China"—has 50,000 visitors every day. Enormous malls in the Philippines, Dubai, and Malaysia have roller coasters, ice-skating rinks, water parks, aquariums, and bowling alleys.

Source: <u>forbes.com</u>

About the Authors

Joan Saslow

Joan Saslow has taught in a variety of programs in South America and the United States. She is author of a number of multi-level integrated-skills courses for adults and young adults: *Ready to Go: Language, Lifeskills, and Civics; Workplace Plus: Living and Working in English;* and of *Literacy Plus.* She is also author of *English in Context: Reading Comprehension for Science and Technology.* Ms. Saslow was the series director of *True Colors* and *True Voices.* She participates in the English Language Specialist Program in the U.S. Department of State's Bureau of Educational and Cultural Affairs.

Allen Ascher

Allen Ascher has been a teacher and a teacher trainer in China and the United States and taught in the TESOL Certificate Program at the New School in New York. He was also academic director of the International English Language Institute at Hunter College. Mr. Ascher is author of the "Teaching Speaking" module of *Teacher Development Interactive,* an online multimedia teacher-training program, and of *Think about Editing: A Grammar Editing Guide for ESL.*

Both Ms. Saslow and Mr. Ascher are frequent and popular speakers at professional conferences and international gatherings of EFL and ESL teachers.

Authors' Acknowledgments

The authors are indebted to these reviewers who provided extensive and detailed feedback and suggestions for the second edition of *Top Notch* as well as the hundreds of teachers who participated in surveys and focus groups.

Manuel Aguilar Díaz, El Cultural Trujillo, Peru • **Manal Al Jordi,** Expression Training Company, Kuwait • **José Luis Ames Portocarrero,** El Cultural Arequipa, Peru • **Vanessa de Andrade,** CCBEU Inter Americano, Curitiba, Brazil • **Rossana Aragón Castro,** ICPNA Cusco, Peru • **Jennifer Ballesteros,** Universidad del Valle de México, Campus Tlalpan, Mexico City, Mexico • **Brad Bawtinheimer,** PROULEX, Guadalajara, Mexico • **Carolina Bermeo,** Universidad Central, Bogotá, Colombia • **Zulma Buitrago,** Universidad Pedagógica Nacional, Bogotá, Colombia • **Fabiola R. Cabello,** Idiomas Católica, Lima, Peru • **Emma Campo Collante,** Universidad Central Bogotá, Colombia • **Viviane de Cássia Santos Carlini,** Spectrum Line, Pouso Alegre, Brazil • **Fanny Castelo,** ICPNA Cusco, Peru • **José Luis Castro Moreno,** Universidad de León, Mexico • **Mei Chia-Hong,** Southern Taiwan University (STUT), Taiwan • **Guven Ciftci,** Faith University, Turkey • **Freddy Correa Montenegro,** Centro Colombo Americano, Cali, Colombia • **Alicia Craman de Carmand,** Idiomas Católica, Lima, Peru • **Jesús G. Díaz Osío,** Florida National College, Miami, USA • **Ruth Domínguez,** Universidad Central Bogotá, Colombia • **Roxana Echave,** El Cultural Arequipa, Peru • **Angélica Escobar Chávez,** Universidad de León, Mexico • **John Fieldeldy,** College of Engineering, Nihon University, Aizuwakamatsu-shi, Japan • **Herlinda Flores,** Centro de Idiomas Universidad Veracruzana, Mexico • **Claudia Franco,** Universidad Pedagógica Nacional, Colombia • **Andrea Fredricks,** Embassy CES, San Francisco, USA • **Chen-Chen Fu,** National Kaoshiung First Science Technology University, Taiwan • **María Irma Gallegos Peláez,** Universidad del Valle de México, Mexico City, Mexico • **Carolina García Carbajal,** El Cultural Arequipa, Peru • **Claudia Gavancho Terrazas,** ICPNA Cusco, Peru • **Adriana Gómez,** Centro Colombo Americano, Bogotá, Colombia • **Raphaël Goossens,** ICPNA Cusco, Peru • **Carlo Granados,** Universidad Central, Bogotá, Colombia • **Ralph Grayson,** Idiomas Católica, Lima, Peru • **Murat Gultekin,** Faith University, Turkey • **Monika Hennessey,** ICPNA Chiclayo, Peru • **Lidia Hernández Medina,** Universidad del Valle de México, Mexico City, Mexico • **Jesse Huang,** National Central University, Taiwan • **Eric Charles Jones,** Seoul University of Technology, South Korea • **Jun-Chen Kuo,** Tajen University, Taiwan • **Susan Krieger,** Embassy CES, San Francisco, USA • **Robert Labelle,** Centre for Training and Development, Dawson College, Canada • **Erin Lemaistre,** Chung-Ang University, South Korea • **Eleanor S. Leu,** Soochow University, Taiwan • **Yihui Li (Stella Li),** Fooyin University, Taiwan • **Chin-Fan Lin,** Shih Hsin University, Taiwan • **Linda Lin,** Tatung Institute of Technology, Taiwan • **Kristen Lindblom,** Embassy CES, San Francisco, USA • **Ricardo López,** PROULEX, Guadalajara, Mexico • **Neil Macleod,** Kansai Gaidai University, Osaka, Japan • **Robyn McMurray,** Pusan National University, South Korea • **Paula Medina,** London Language Institute, Canada • **María Teresa Meléndez de Elorreaga,** ICPNA Chiclayo, Peru • **Sandra Cecilia Mora Espejo,** Universidad del Valle de México, Campus Tlalpan, Mexico City, Mexico • **Ricardo Nausa,** Centro Colombo Americano, Bogotá, Colombia • **Tim Newfields,** Tokyo University Faculty of Economics, Tokyo, Japan • **Mónica Nomberto,** ICPNA Chiclayo, Peru • **Scarlett Ostojic,** Idiomas Católica, Lima, Peru • **Ana Cristina Ochoa,** CCBEU Inter Americano, Curitiba, Brazil • **Doralba Pérez,** Universidad Pedagógica Nacional, Bogotá, Colombia • **David Perez Montalvo,** ICPNA Cusco, Peru • **Wahrena Elizabeth Pfeister,** University of Suwon, South Korea • **Wayne Allen Pfeister,** University of Suwon, South Korea • **Cecilia Ponce de León,** ICPNA Cusco, Peru • **Andrea Rebonato,** CCBEU Inter Americano, Curitiba, Brazil • **Elizabeth Rodríguez López,** El Cultural Trujillo, Peru • **Olga Rodríguez Romero,** El Cultural Trujillo, Peru • **Timothy Samuelson,** BridgeEnglish, Denver, USA • **Enrique Sánchez Guzmán,** PROULEX, Guadalajara, Mexico • **Letícia Santos,** ICBEU Ibiá, Brazil • **Lyndsay Shaeffer,** Embassy CES, San Francisco, USA • **John Eric Sherman,** Hong Ik University, South Korea • **João Vitor Soares,** NACC, São Paulo, Brazil • **Elena Sudakova,** English Language Center, Kiev, Ukraine • **Richard Swingle,** Kansai Gaidai College, Osaka, Japan • **Sandrine Ting,** St. John's University, Taiwan • **Shu-Ping Tsai,** Fooyin University, Taiwan • **José Luis Urbina Hurtado,** Universidad de León, Mexico • **Monica Urteaga,** Idiomas Católica, Lima, Peru • **Juan Carlos Villafuerte,** ICPNA Cusco, Peru • **Dr. Wen-hsien Yang,** National Kaohsiung Hospitality College, Kaohsiung, Taiwan • **Holger Zamora,** ICPNA Cusco, Peru.